Presents

Master Rock GUITAR

Written & Method By:
John McCarthy

Adapted By: Jimmy Rutkowski & Steve Gorenberg
Supervising Editor: John McCarthy
Music Transcribing & Engraving: Jimmy Rutkowski
Production Manager: John McCarthy
Layout, Graphics & Design: Jimmy Rutkowski
Photography: Rodney Dabney
Copy Editor: Cathy McCarthy

Cover Art Direction & Design:
Jimmy Rutkowski

HL14041716
ISBN: 978-1-4584-2323-8
Produced by The Rock House Method®
© 2013 McCarthy Publishing, LLC All Rights Reserved

Table of Contents

About the Author 4
Icon Key 5
Digital eBook... 5

DVD 1

Parts of the Guitar 6
Holding the Guitar & Pick 7
Names of the Open Strings & Tuning 9
Reading Chord Charts 9
Major Open Chords 10
Picking Exercise 13
Basic Strumming 14
Tablature Explanation 17
Finger Exercise #1 19
Blues Rhythm #1 20
Minor Open Chords 22
Open Chord Rhythm 24
Finger Exercise #2 25
How to Read a Scale Diagram 26
Minor Pentatonic Scales 1 - 3 27
Double Lead Pattern 28
Introduction to Bending 29
Bar Chords 30
Bar Chord Rhythm #1 32
Bar Chord Rhythm #2 33
Rock Riffs 34
Hammer On & Pull Off Exercise 35
Full Blues Rhythm & Lead 36
Single String Picking 38
Minor Pentatonic Scales 4 - 5 38
Triplet Lead Pattern 40
Rock Rhythm & Lead 42
Review Quiz 1 44
Guitar Solo 46
Review Open Chords 52

DVD 2

Review Pentatonic Scales 56
Lead Patterns 58
Bending Exercise 62
Bar Chords 63
Rhythms To Play Scales & Patterns Over 65
Workout Section 67
Blues Rhythm & Lead 72
Blues Scales 76
Arpeggios 78
Rock Rhythm & Melodic Lead 80
Multi-Position Lead Pattern 82
Bi-Dextral Hammer Ons 83
Natural Minor Scales 84
Drop D Tuning 86
Slow Metal Rhythm & Solo 88
Review Quiz 2 90
Changing a String 92
Guitar Accessories 94
Review Quiz Answers 96

Words from the Author

Playing guitar is a rewarding art form that will last you a lifetime. I have spent my career sharing the passion I have for guitar with others. If you follow my guitar method step-by-step you will be successful and enjoy playing guitar for years to come. When I designed The Rock House Method, my mission was to create the most complete, easy and fun way to learn. I accomplished this by developing and systematically arranging a modern method based on the needs and social demands of today's players. I not only tell you where to put your fingers, I show you ways to use what you learn so that you can make music right from the start. I know it is hard to imagine, but even the all-time greats started somewhere, there was a time when they too didn't even know what a chord was. As you progress as a guitar player, keep your mind open to all styles of music. Set-up a practice schedule that you can manage, be consistent, challenge yourself and realize everyone learns at a different rate. Be patient, persistent and remember music is supposed to be fun!

Now, GET EXCITED! YOU are going to play guitar!

John McCarthy

About the Author

John McCarthy
Creator of
The Rock House Method

John is the creator of The Rock House Method®, the world's leading musical instruction system. Over his 30 plus year career, he has written, produced and/or appeared in more than 100 instructional products. Millions of people around the world have learned to play music using John's easy-to-follow, accelerated programs.

John is a virtuoso musician who has worked with some of the industry's most legendary entertainers. He has the ability to break down, teach and communicate music in a manner that motivates and inspires others to achieve their dreams of playing an instrument.

As a musician and songwriter, John blends together a unique style of rock, metal, funk and blues in a collage of melodic compositions. Throughout his career, John has recorded and performed with renowned musicians including Doug Wimbish (Joe Satriani, Living Colour, The Rolling Stones, Madonna, Annie Lennox), Grammy Winner Leo Nocentelli, Rock & Roll Hall of Fame inductees Bernie Worrell and Jerome "Big Foot" Brailey, Freekbass, Gary Hoey, Bobby Kimball, David Ellefson (founding member of seven time Grammy nominee Megadeth), Will Calhoun (B.B. King, Mick Jagger and Paul Simon), Gus G of Ozzy and many more.

To get more information about John McCarthy, his music and his instructional products visit RockHouseSchool.com.

Icon Key

These tell you there is additional information and learning utilities available at RockHouseSchool.com to support that lesson.

Backing Track

Many of the exercises in this book are intended to be played along with bass and drum rhythm tracks. This icon indicates that there is a backing track available for download on the *Lesson Support* site.

Metronome

Metronome icons are placed next to the examples that we recommend you practice using a metronome. You can download a free, adjustable metronome on the *Lesson Support* site.

Tuner

You can download the free online tuner on the *Lesson Support* site to help tune your instrument.

Additional Information

The question mark icon indicates there is more information for that section available on the Lesson Support site. It can be theory, more playing examples or tips.

Digital eBook

When you register this product at the lesson support site RockHouseSchool.com, you will receive a digital version of this book. This interactive e-Book can be used on all devices that support Adobe PDF. This will allow you to access your book using the latest portable technology any time you want.

DVD 1
Parts of the Guitar

The guitar is divided into three main sections: the body, the neck and the headstock. The guitar's input jack will be located on the side or front of the body. The assembly that anchors the strings to the body is called the bridge. The saddles hold the strings properly in place; the height of each string (or action) can be adjusted with the saddle. Mounted to the body behind the strings are the pickups. A pickup functions like the guitar's microphone; it picks up the vibrations of the strings and converts them to a signal that travels through the guitar cord to the amplifier. Also located on the front of the body are the volume and tone knobs and the pickup selector switch or toggle switch. Strap buttons are located on both sides of the body where a guitar strap can be attached. The front face of the neck is called the fretboard (or fingerboard). The metal bars going across the fretboard are called frets. The dots are position markers (or fret markers) for visual reference to help you gauge where you are on the neck while playing. The nut is the string guide that holds the strings in place where the neck meets the headstock. The headstock contains the machine heads (also referred to as tuners); the machine heads are used to tune the strings by tightening or loosening them.

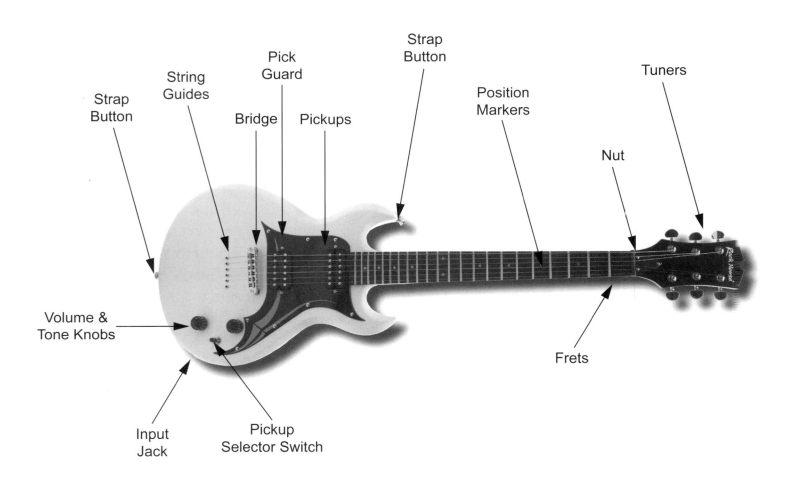

Holding the Guitar & Pick

Throughout this book, we will refer to the picking hand as your right hand, and the fretting hand as your left hand, left handed players take note. While sitting or standing always angle the guitar neck up at a 30 degree angle. Find a comfortable chair with no arms where your feet are flat on the floor.

Holding the Guitar

Attaching Your Strap

To stand up and play you must attach a strap to your guitar. Most electric and acoustic guitars have strap buttons on both sides of the guitar body to attach the strap. Some acoustic guitars don't have a strap button on the neck side of the body. Attach the strap with a string tying it around the neck after the nut of the guitar on the headstock. Don't adjust the strap too low and keep a consistent guitar position sitting and standing. You should always have the neck of your guitar pointed up at about a 30 degree angle to ensure proper hand position.

Holding the Pick

Center the pick on the index finger of your right hand. Bring your thumb down on top of the pick. Pinch your thumb and finger together and leave just the tip of the pick showing. Leave your hand open and your other fingers relaxed (don't make a fist).

  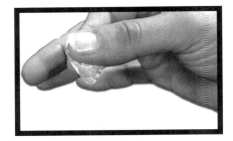

Right Hand Position

Place your right hand forearm on the top of the guitar body. Drape your arm and hand over the strings almost parallel with the bridge. Anchor one or more of your fingers onto the guitar body. This will help gauge your pick placement.

Left Hand Position

Hold your left hand in front of the neck, wrist straight and curl your fingers in to make a "C" shape with your hand. Bring your hand to the neck in a comfortable and natural fashion. Be sure to place your thumb in the middle of the back of the neck. If your wrist is bent raise the guitar neck higher until it is straight.

Names of the Open Strings & Tuning

The fattest string is the 6th string and the thinnest is the 1st string. A great way to remember the open strings is to use an acronym creating a word for each letter name. The following is a silly acronym I created: Every – Bad – Girl – Deserves – Another – Egg. Make up you own saying for the open strings.

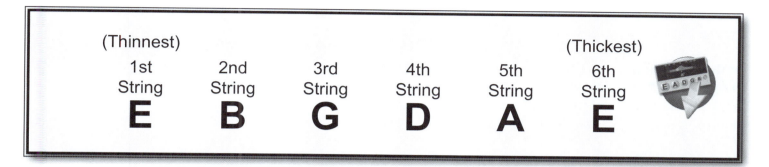

Tuning

Tune your guitar using the machine heads on the headstock. Tighten the string to raise the pitch. Loosen the string to lower the pitch. Be careful not to accidentally break a string by tightening it too much or too quickly. The easiest way to tune a guitar is to use an electronic tuner. You can download your free online tuner from RockHouseMethod.com.

Reading Chord Charts

A chord is a group of notes played together. A chord chart (chord diagram) is a graphic representation of part of the fretboard (as if you stood the guitar up from floor to ceiling and looked directly at the front of the neck). The vertical lines represent the strings; the horizontal lines represent the frets.

Chord diagrams show which notes to play and which strings they are played on. The solid black dots within the graph represent fretted notes and show you where your fingers should go. Each of these dots will have a number directly below it, underneath the diagram. These numbers indicate which left hand finger to fret the note with (1 = index, 2 = middle, 3 = ring, 4 = pinky). The 0s at the bottom of the diagram show which strings are played open (strummed with no left hand fingers touching them).

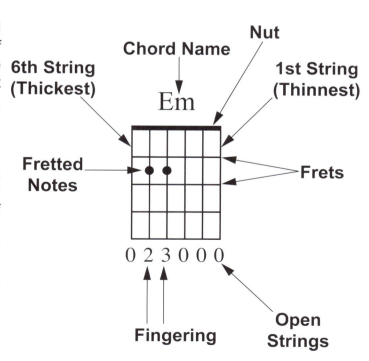

Major Open Chords

Now that you know how to read a chord diagram, it's time to learn your first chords. The following seven chords are all open chords because they either contain open strings or are played in open position (at or near the 1st fret of the guitar). For each chord, the first photo shows what the chord looks like from the front. The second photo is from the player's perspective. Major chords are represented in this book using a capital letter by itself for the chord name. They can also be shown using the letter name followed by a capital letter M, Maj, or Major.

In the A chord diagram, the slur going across the notes means you should bar (bar) those notes. A bar is executed by placing one finger flat across more than one string. Pick each note of the chord individually to make sure you're applying enough pressure with your finger. Notice that the 6th and 1st strings each have an "x" below them on the diagram, indicating these strings are not played (either muted or not strummed).

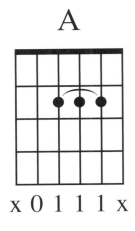

Let's start off with a simple down-strum. Fret the A chord with your left hand. Starting from the 5th string, lightly drag the pick downward across the strings in a smooth motion. The strumming motion should come from your elbow and wrist. When strumming chords, pivot from your elbow and keep your wrist straight. When playing single notes, use more wrist. You may find the bar to be somewhat difficult to execute at first, however this is a very common technique used to fret many chords on the guitar and it's important to master this technique early on. Be careful not to accidentally bar or strum the 1st string; this string should be muted or not played.

Now let's move on to the B and C chords. The B chord is slightly more difficult to play and requires you to really stretch your hand out in order to properly fret all of the notes. When fretting the C chord, make sure that your fingers aren't accidentally muting the required open strings. Remember to keep your thumb firmly anchored against the back of the neck. Your fingers should be curled inward toward the fretboard and only the tips of your fingers should be touching the strings. Don't grab the neck with your whole hand; no other parts of your fingers or hand should be touching the neck or any of the other strings. Place your fingertips just to the left of (behind) the fret, pressing the strings inward toward the neck.

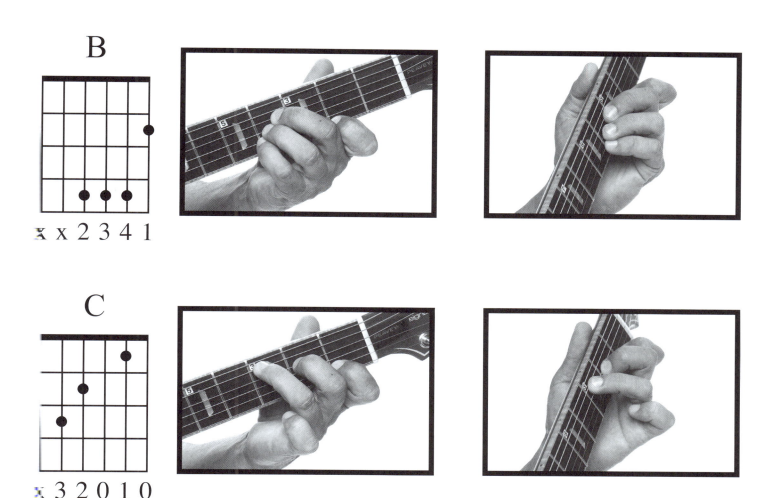

One of the hardest things for a beginner to conquer is the ability to play a clean, fully sustained chord without buzzing strings, muted or dead notes. Make sure your left hand is fretting the proper notes and your fingers aren't accidentally touching any of the other strings. Pick each string individually with your right hand, one note at a time. If any of the open strings are deadened or muted, try slightly adjusting your fingers. If any of the fretted notes are buzzing, you probably aren't pressing down hard enough with your fingers. It will be difficult at first and might hurt a little, but don't get discouraged. With time and practice, you'll build up callouses on your fingertips. Before you know it, playing chords will be second nature and your fingers will hardly feel it at all.

The D and E chords are easier to play than the previous chords. They are also two of the most commonly used open major chords. Neither chord uses the fourth finger and all of the fretted notes are on adjacent strings, making it easier to play them cleanly.

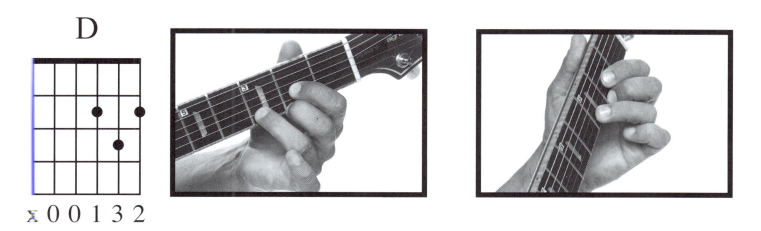

E

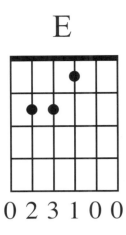
0 2 3 1 0 0

The last two open major chords in this section are the F and G chords. The F chord is especially difficult to play because you need to bar the highest two strings with your first finger and put your second and third fingers down straight. If you tilt your first finger bar to the left side, it makes it easier to fret the other notes properly. Pick each note out individually to make sure the chord sounds clean and that you're playing it correctly. Once you've memorized all of the open major chords, practice changing from chord to chord efficiently.

F

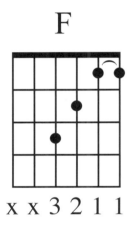
x x 3 2 1 1

G

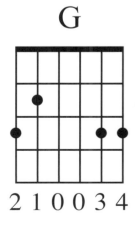
2 1 0 0 3 4

Picking Exercise

Picking Symbols

There are two different ways to pick a string: down or up. The symbols below are used to indicate a down pick or an up pick. Practice picking down and up on the 6th string for a few minutes.

⊓ = Down Pick (Toward the Floor)

V = Up Pick (Toward the Ceiling)

An easy way of remembering which symbol is which in the beginning, is to realize that the open side of each symbol is in the direction of the pick stroke that it represents.

Here's an alternate picking exercise to help coordinate your right hand. Instead of strumming the chords, you might pick the notes of a chord out individually and let them ring out together.

Fret an open D chord and hold the chord shape with your left hand while picking out the individual notes in the order indicated below. This picking pattern (indicated by which number string you pick) is 4 - 1 - 3 - 1 - 2 - 1. Recite the string number while you pick each one to help memorize the order. Use a down-up-down-up alternate picking pattern. Notice that the 1st string is always up-picked, while the other strings are all down-picked. Try to hold one of your right hand fingers on the body of the guitar to help give you added support and control. Practice playing in a steady, even rhythm, in time with a metronome.

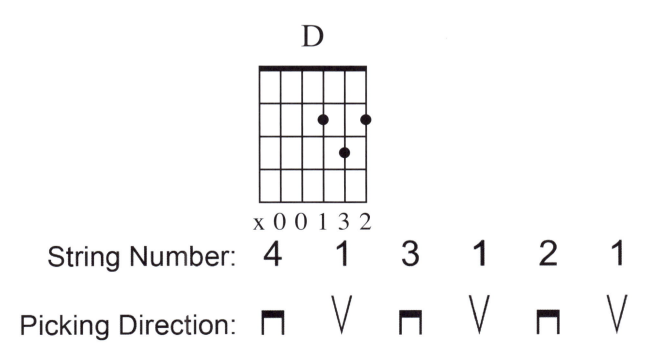

13

Basic Strumming

Once you have the chords sounding clean and the strumming motion down, the next step is to learn how to change chords quickly and cleanly. Focus on where each finger needs to move for the next chord. Sometimes one or more of your fingers will be able to stay in the same place. Avoid taking your hand completely off the neck. Instead, try to move your whole hand as little as possible and make smaller finger adjustments to change from one chord to the next. When you can change from chord to chord seemlessly, you'll be able to play complete songs.

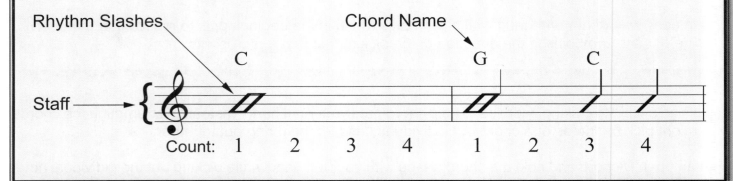

Strumming Pattern #1

In this chord progression, strum each chord four times, using all down-strums. This example also uses repeat signs (play through the progression and repeat it again). Keep practicing and try to change chords in time without stalling or missing a beat. Count along out loud with each strum, in time and on the beat. Start out slowly if you need to and gradually get it up to speed.

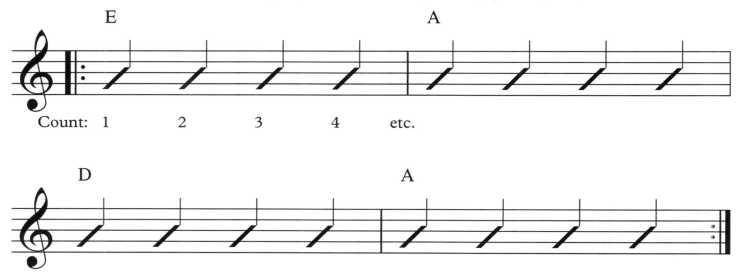

You don't need to read traditional music notation in order to play guitar, but it's helpful to understand a little bit about the concept of rhythm and timing. In most popular rock and blues, music is divided into measures of four beats. When a band counts off "One, two, three, four" at the beginning of a song, it represents one complete measure of music. Different types of notes are held for different durations within a measure. For example, a quarter note gets one beat because a quarter note is held for one quarter of a measure.

Whole Notes = 4 Beats

This is a Whole Note. The head is hollow and there is no stem or flag. A Whole Note will receive four beats or counts.

Half Notes = 2 Beats

This is a Half Note. The head is hollow and there is a stem. A Half Note will receive two beats or counts.

Quarter Notes = 1 Beat

This is a Quarter Note. The head is solid and there is a stem. A Quarter Note will receive one beat or count.

Eighth Notes = 1/2 Beat

These are Eighth Notes. The head is solid and there is a stem with a flag. An Eighth Note will receive one half beat or count.

One Eighth Note   Two Eighth Notes   Four Eighth Notes

Music notation is the language of music that is shared between instruments. The Rock House Method offers a unique learning system for reading standard notation called "Reading Music for Guitar." Though it is a personal choice to learn to sight read, we strongly feel that in order to become a well rounded musician, you should begin working with "Reading Music for Guitar" as a supplement to your current studies.

The Tie

A tie is a curved line connecting one note to the next. If two notes are tied, strike only the first one and let it ring out through the duration of the second note (or "tied" note).

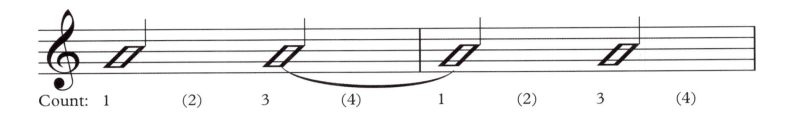

Count: 1   (2)   3   (4)   1   (2)   3   (4)

Dotted Notes

A dot after a note increases its value by another 1/2 of its original value. In the following example the half notes are dotted, so they are held for three beats.

Count: 1   (2   3)   4   1   (2   3)   4

Strumming Pattern #2

The following strumming pattern uses another new chord, the Cadd9 chord. A Cadd9 chord (or a Csus2 chord) is a slight variation of the regular C chord. Notice how similar the fingering is to the G chord and how easy it is to switch back and forth between them. Just leave your third and fourth fingers stationary and move your first and second fingers up or down one string.

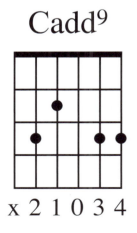

This exercise utilizes a strumming technique that we call a ghost strum. A ghost strum occurs when you move the pick over the strings without actually striking them. This allows you to keep your arm moving in a constant down-up-down motion, keeping your playing fluid and in time. The strumming symbols in parentheses indicate where ghost strums occur. The rhythm used is an example of syncopation. You're playing a syncopated rhythm if there's one or more strums off the beat, or on the upbeat instead of the downbeat. The strum on beat 2 1/2 is tied to beat 3, so you don't strum directly on beat 3. If you're having trouble changing from chord to chord smoothly, isolate the change and just practice going back and forth between those two chords. With practice, you'll build finger memory and your fingers will instinctively know where to go. Play this rhythm along with the backing track and get the changes, the feel and the strumming motion down.

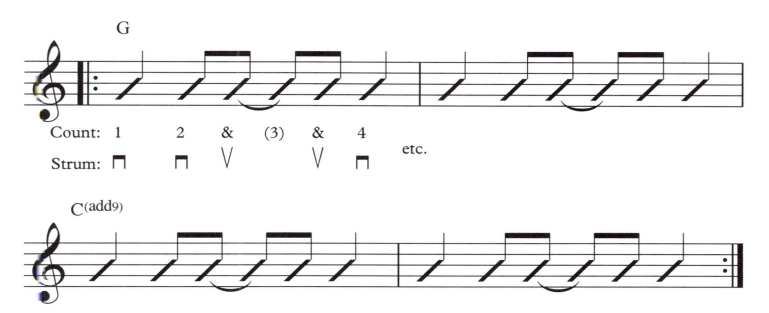

Tablature Explanation

Tablature (or tab) is a number system for reading notes on the guitar. The six lines of the tablature staff represent each of the strings on the guitar. The top line is the thinnest (highest pitched) string. The numbers placed directly on these lines are the fret number to play each note. Underneath the staff, is a series of numbers that tell you which left hand finger to fret the notes with. The tablature staff is divided into a small sections called measures by bar lines.

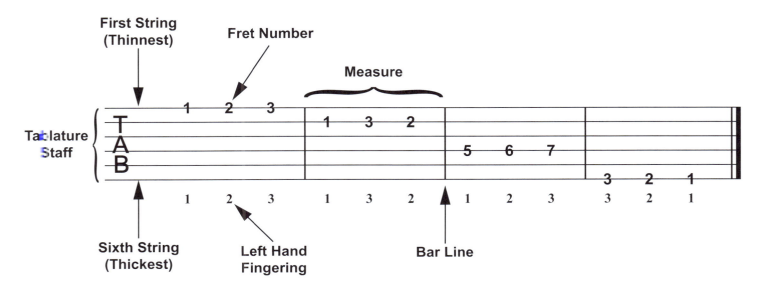

17

Chords in Tablature

Chords can also be written in tab. If there are several numbers stacked together in a column, those notes should be played or strummed at the same time. Here are the seven major open chords you already know from the previous section with the tablature written out underneath each diagram. Since the fingerings are shown on the chord diagrams, we won't bother to repeat them underneath the tab.

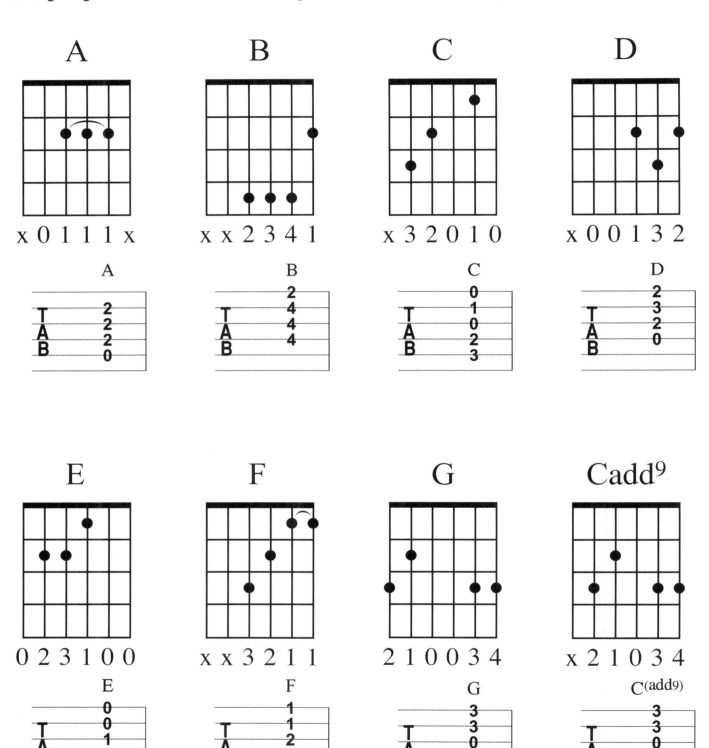

18

Finger Exercise #1

This is a finger exercise in tablature that will build coordination and strengthen your fingers. It's designed to help stretch your hand out, so keep your fingers spread across the first four frets, one finger per fret. Leave your first finger anchored in place and reach for the following three notes by stretching your hand out.

With your right hand, use alternate picking in a consistent down-up-down-up pendulum motion. Alternate picking will help develop speed, smoothness and technique. Practice this exercise using the metronome for timing and control.

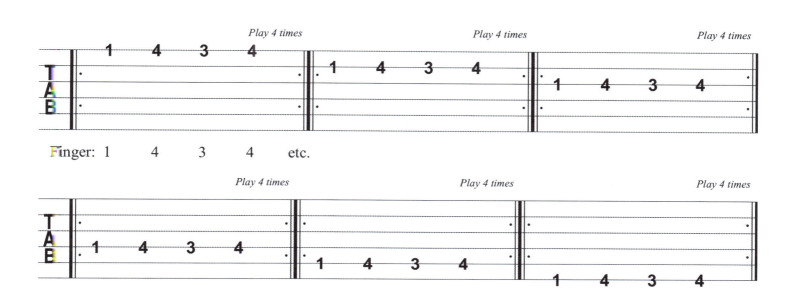

Quick Tip!
Choosing A Teacher

Finding a good guitar teacher is essential, especially for beginners. Playing well and teaching well are separate skills. Just because someone can play guitar doesn't automatically mean they have the proper skills to teach guitar. Before you commit to a teacher, you may want to ask for a trial lesson to make sure you're happy with the communication skills and the teaching method the instructor provides. If you're not learning from someone who knows how to teach, you may have a difficult time.

Blues Rhythm #1

The following is a basic blues riff in the key of A. This riff is made up of two note chords shown on the tab staff. The chord names above the staff are there as a reference to show you what the basic harmony is while you play along.

This riff should sound very familiar - it's used more than any other blues progression. Plenty of rock and blues classics are played entirely with this one riff repeated over and over. It is made up of 12 measures (or bars) of music called the 12-bar blues, a blues progression consisting of twelve repeated bars of music.

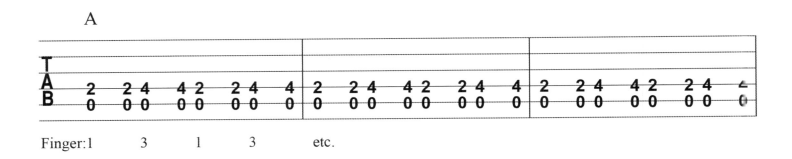

Finger: 1   3   1   3   etc.

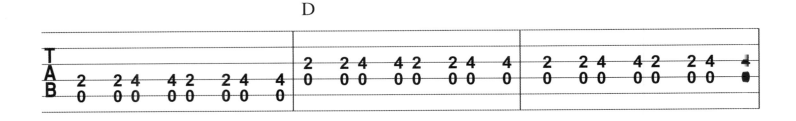

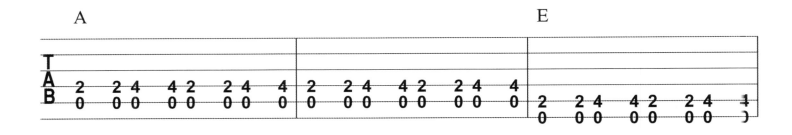

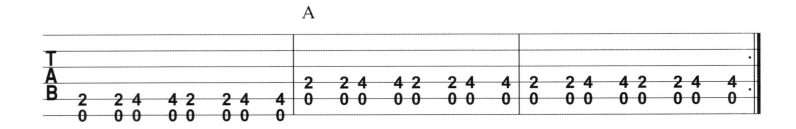

20

Blues is played with a shuffle feel, also called a triplet feel. This example was written in eighth notes and the second eighth note of each beat should lag a little. This is referred to as triplet feel because the beat is actually divided by thirds, counted as if there were three eighth notes per beat instead of two. The first part of the beat gets 2/3 of a beat and the second part only gets 1/3.

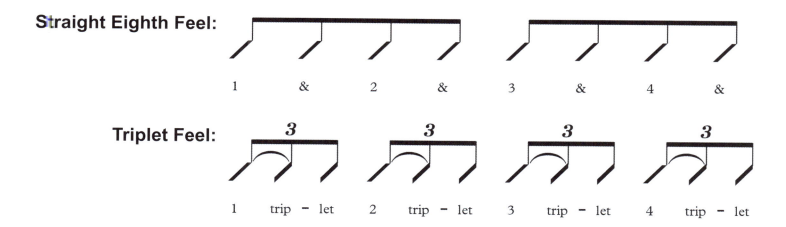

Shuffle feel is a much easier concept to understand by hearing it. Listen to the backing track, count along and try to get the triplet feel in your head. Also, check out almost any blues standard, slow or fast and you'll probably recognize a shuffle feel being used.

This 12-bar blues riff is also an example of a I - IV - V (one - four - five) chord progression. The Roman numerals refer to the steps of the scale, relative to what key the music is in. This blues riff is in the key of A, so the A chord is the I chord (also called the tonic). The D chord is the IV chord (also called the subdominant) because in the key of A, D is the fourth step of the scale. Finally, the V chord (or dominant) is the E chord, because E is the fifth step of the scale in the key of A.

The I - IV - V chord progression is the most common progression used in rock or blues. It's the foundation that all rock and blues was built on and has evolved from. There are many variations, but songs such as "Johnny B. Goode," "You Really Got Me," "Rock and Roll," "I Love Rock and Roll" and "Sympathy for the Devil" are all based on the I - IV - V.

Quick Tip!

Always Tune Your Guitar

Make sure your guitar is in tune every time you play it. You could be playing all of the right notes, but they'll sound incorrect if you haven't tuned up. Even if only one string is slightly out of tune, the simplest of chords will sound bad. It's a good idea to stop and check your tuning from time to time while practicing.

Minor Open Chords

Minor chords have a sad or melancholy sound, whereas major chords have a happy or bright sound. In this section we'll learn the seven popular minor open (or 1st position) chords. A lowercase "m" within a chord name indicates a minor chord.

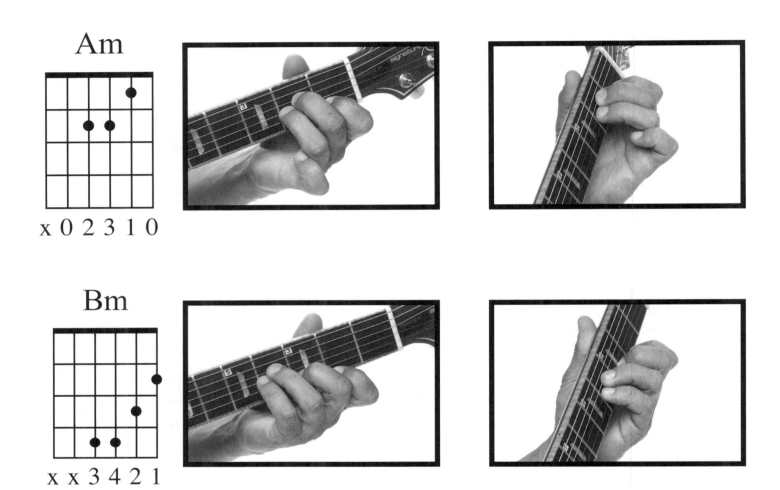

Notice that the Bm and Cm chords both have the exact same fingering. To go from Bm to Cm, simply slide your hand up the neck one fret to the 3rd fret (indicated by the 3fr. just to the left of the Cm chord diagram).

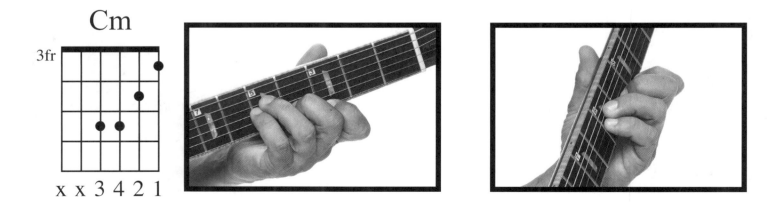

Dm

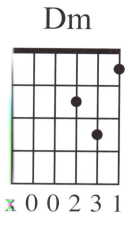 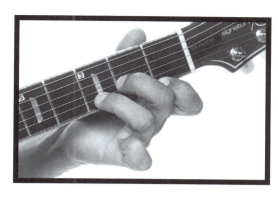 

x 0 0 2 3 1

Em

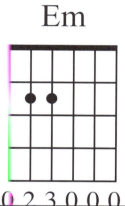  

0 2 3 0 0 0

E Minor Alternate Fingering

Here's an alternate fingering for the Em chord using the first and second fingers. Depending on the context in which it's used in a chord progression, it might be easier to change from chord to chord by slightly varying the fingering. Both fingerings of the chord are useful to know.

Em

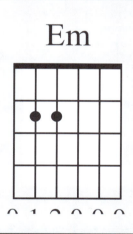

0 1 2 0 0 0

The Fm and Gm chords contain a first finger bar and also use identical fingerings; Fm is played at the 1st fret, and Gm is played one whole step higher at the 3rd fret.

Fm

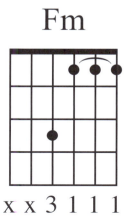  

x x 3 1 1 1

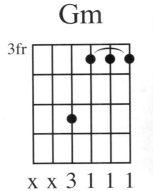

Open Chord Rhythm

This chord progression combines both major and minor chords in the key of A minor. The four chords used in the progression are shown in order using chord diagrams below. Use the alternate fingering for the Em chord (with your first and second fingers) to make changing from chord to chord easier. Notice how similar the fingerings are between the Am and C chords; simply move your third finger and leave your other fingers stationary. Play along with the backing track and practice changing chords clearly and in time. Use the strumming pattern indicated by the symbols above the tab staff.

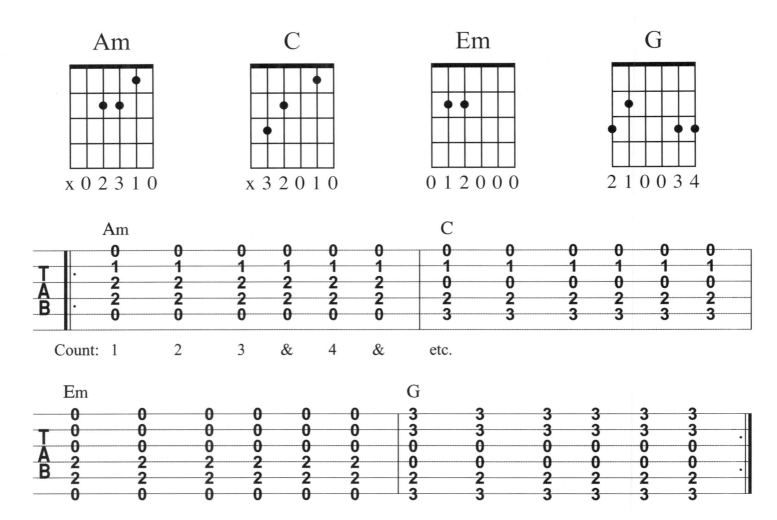

Major & Minor Sounds

You will learn major and minor chords in this book. Major chords have a happy or bright sound. Minor chords have a sad or melancholy sound. If someone was writing a song about the happiest day of their life they would use major chords. But if they were writing a song about a friend moving away they would surely use minor chords.

Finger Exercise #2

This is a finger exercise in tablature that will build coordination and strengthen your left hand. Fret each note individually, using one finger at a time. Play each measure four times, then proceed to the next measure without pausing. This will help build endurance. Use alternate picking and practice this exercise using the metronome for timing and control.

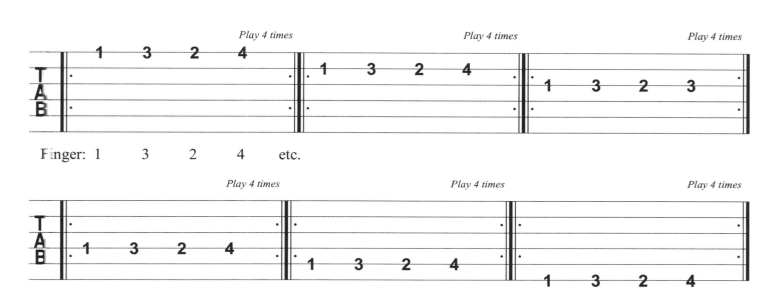

Quick Tip!

Make Sure Your Guitar Is Set Up Properly

Beginners don't usually realize that their new guitars may need to be set up to play comfortably. A proper set up will ensure that the strings are at the correct height. If they're too high off the neck, it will be harder to press the strings down. You'll also want to check the neck adjustment to be sure your guitar neck has the proper curve. Even right out of the box, new guitars need adjusting. This oversight can cause many beginners to give up in frustration before giving it a fair chance on a properly adjusted instrument.

How to Read a Scale Diagram

Scale diagrams are simply a diagram outlining where the notes of a scale are located on the guitar neck. The six lines that go from top to bottom represent each of the six strings. The dots placed directly on a string show you the specific fret to play each note, and the number below the dots string indicates which left hand finger to fret the note with. The number to the left of the diagram indicates where on the neck the scale is located, in this diagram the scale begins at the 5th fret:

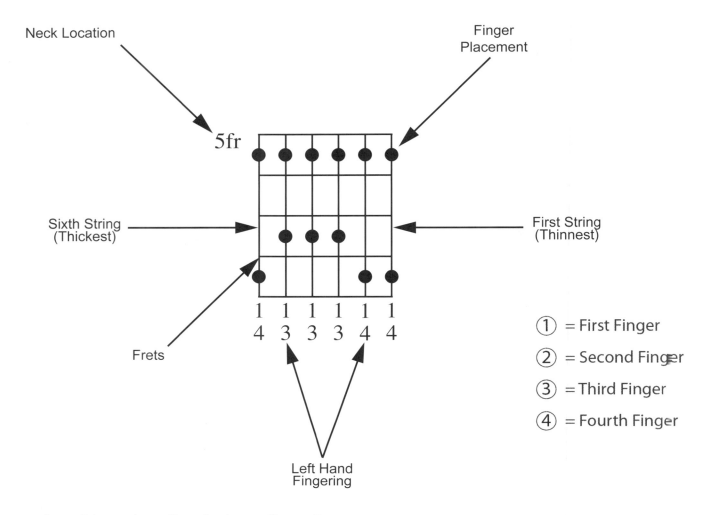

Below see how this scale pattern looks on the guitar:

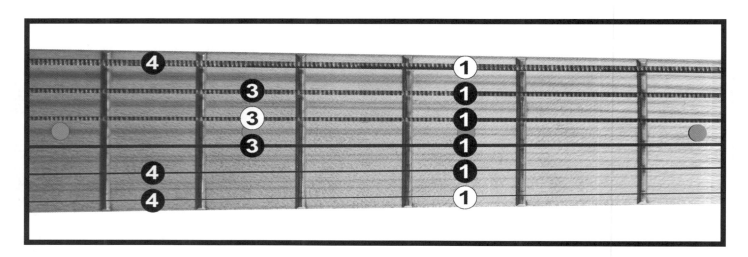

Minor Pentatonic Scales 1 - 3

Minor pentatonic scales are the most commonly used scales for playing rock and blues solos. The pentatonic is a five note scale, or an abbreviated version of the full natural minor scale. The word "pentatonic" comes from the greek words, "penta" (five) and "tonic" (the keynote).

Here is the A minor pentatonic scale shown in tab. Practice the scale ascending and descending using consistent alternate picking. Memorize this scale; it's the one you'll use most often for playing melodies and leads.

1st Position A Minor Pentatonic - Ascending

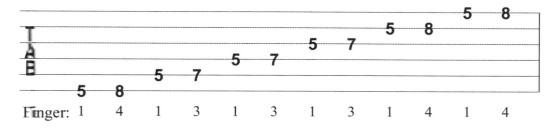
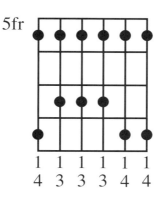

1st Position A Minor Pentatonic - Descending

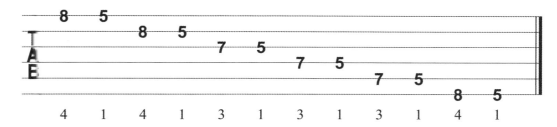

2nd Position A Minor Pentatonic

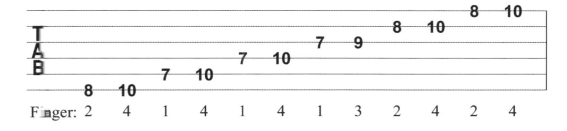
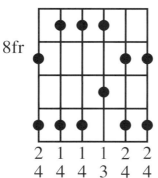

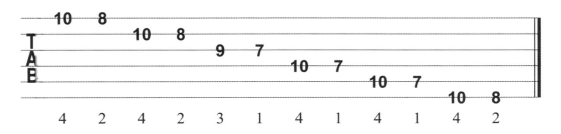

3rd Position A Minor Pentatonic

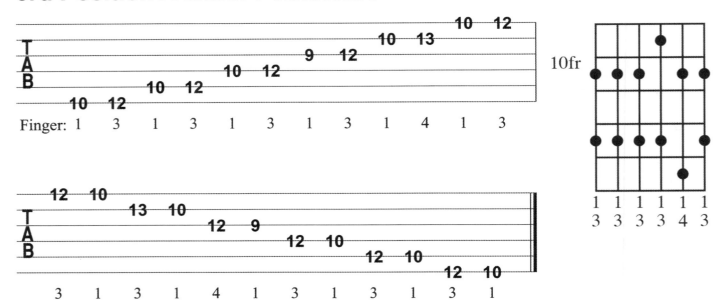

Double Lead Pattern

The following example is a standard lead pattern exercise, designed to help you build coordination and learn how to begin using the minor pentatonics for playing leads. Use alternate picking and the metronome to start out slowly and get the rhythm. Memorize the pattern and gradually speed up the tempo. Before you know it, you'll be playing blazing rock and blues guitar solos.

Here is the 1st position A minor pentatonic scale played using a doubling pattern. Play the notes on the 5th through 2nd strings twice as you travel up and down the scale. Use alternate picking and a steady, even tempo.

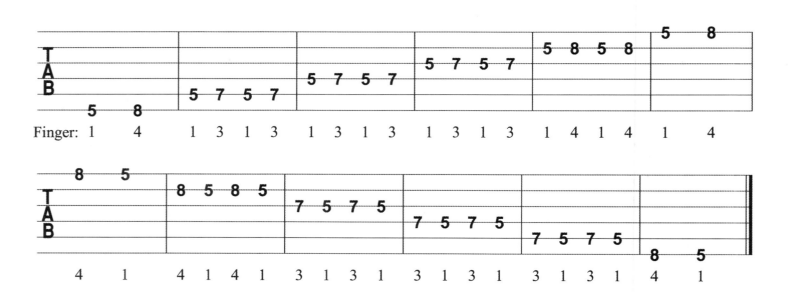

Now let's take the same double lead pattern and transpose it to the 2nd position. Once you've got these two memorized, transpose this pattern to the 3rd position as well.

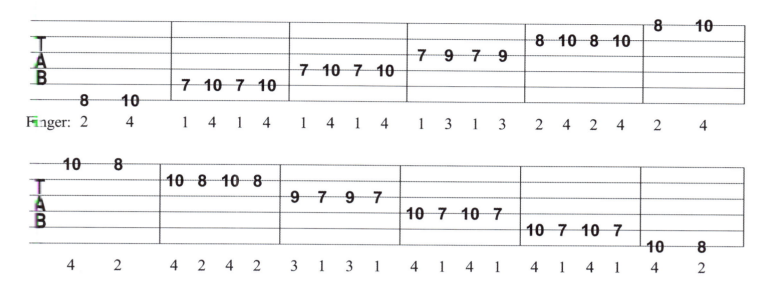

Introduction to Bending

Now let's learn some lead guitar techniques that will add expression to your playing. Bends are a very soulful way of creating emotion with the guitar, using flesh against steel to alter and control pitches. All guitarists have their own unique, signature way of bending notes.

The row of tab staffs below show bends using the third, fourth or first fingers. The "B" above the staff indicates a bend, and the arrow with a "1" above it means to bend the note one whole step in pitch.

First try the third finger bend. While fretting the note with your third finger, keep your first two fingers down on the string behind it and push upward using all three fingers. This will give you added coordination and control. Use the same technique for the fourth finger bend, using all four fingers to bend the string upward. The first finger bend will probably be the hardest since you are only using one finger to bend the string. In some situations, you may even pull the string downward with your first finger to bend the note.

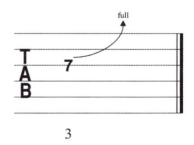

3

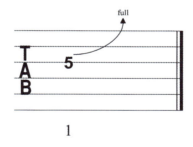

1

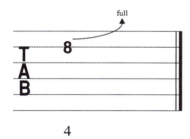

4

The following exercise shows what bending looks like in context when playing a solo using the 1st position A minor pentatonic scale. Play through this exercise and start to get a feel for how to incorporate bends into your own riffs.

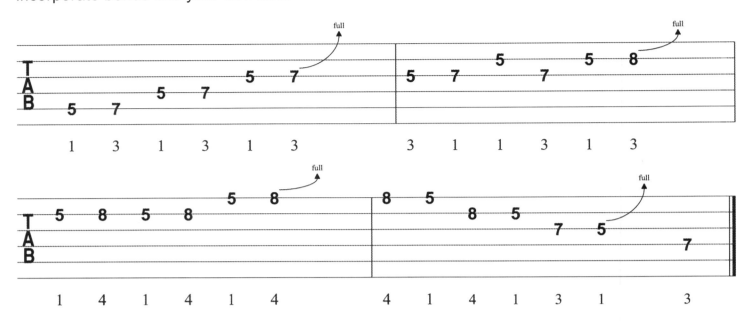

Bar Chords

The F and Bb bar chords contain no open strings. This means you could play them on any fret on the neck. They will change names as you move them from fret to fret. After you have all the notes sounded, move them up the neck one fret at a time to the 12th fret. These are very difficult chords to play, so don't get discouraged if you don't get all the notes to sound when you first try them.

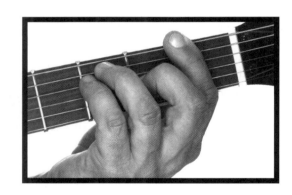

Bar chords have been used in countless songs, they are very important chords to know. The chart below will help guide you to memorize the names of each chord as you move them up the neck. The lowest note of each of these chords is the root note, or the name of that chord.

Name -	F	F#	G	G#	A	A#	B	C	C#	D	D#	E
Fret -	1	2	3	4	5	6	7	8	9	10	11	12
Name -	Bb	B	C	C#	D	D#	E	F	F#	G	G#	A

For the Bb chord, you need to bar across three strings with your third finger. The Fm and Bbm chords are only slightly different. All of these chords are also moveable using the chart.

Fm

1 3 4 1 1 1

Quick Tip: On the Bb chord I touch the tip of my 1st finger on the 6th string to mute it because this note is not in the chord.

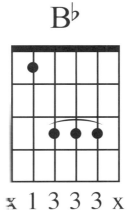

B♭

x 1 3 3 3 x

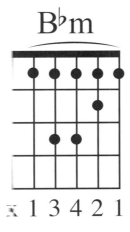

B♭m

x 1 3 4 2 1

Bar Chord Rhythm #1

Rhythms for many rock songs are played using only bar chords. Learning how to comfortably change from chord to chord is essential. The following rhythm uses all bar chords and is played using a typical eighth note strumming pattern. Count along as you play to get the correct timing. Take it slow at first until you master switching from chord to chord in time and on the beat. When you've got it memorized, practice playing along with the bass and drum backing track.

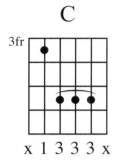
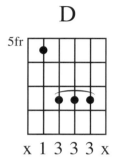
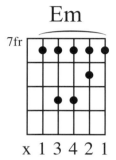
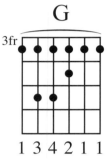

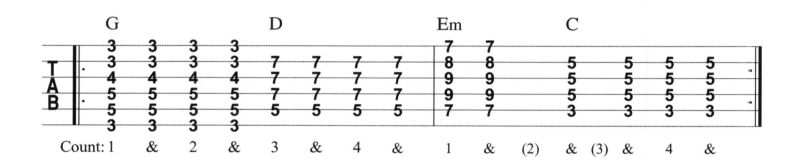

Quick Tip!

Develop Good Practice Habits

Knowing how to practice efficiently will accelerate your progress. Set aside a certain amount of time for practicing and have a routine that reviews all of the techniques you know. Create your own exercises that target weaknesses in your playing. It's important to experiment and get creative as well; try things fast or slow, light or hard, soft or loud.

Bar Chord Rhythm #2

The following example is another popular rock rhythm using all bar chords. Play along to the backing track and get the quick strumming feel down. You can take all of the chords you've learned and play them in this or any other rhythm, then try writing some of your own songs.

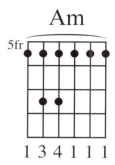

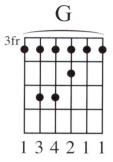

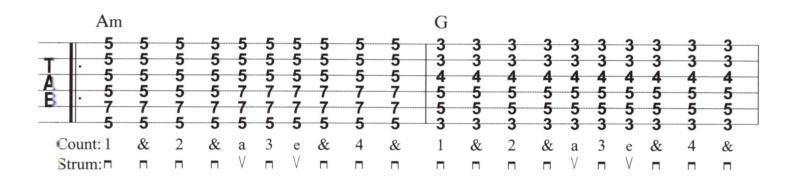

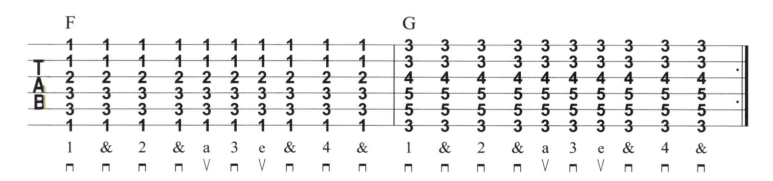

33

Rock Riffs

Here are some familiar rock riff examples. A riff is a repeated theme, usually made up of a series of single notes. Many rock and metal songs are based on one or two simple riffs. In the following examples the left hand fingerings are shown below each tab staff. The second and third riffs have specific picking patterns that are indicated by the picking symbols above each staff.

Rock Riffs 1

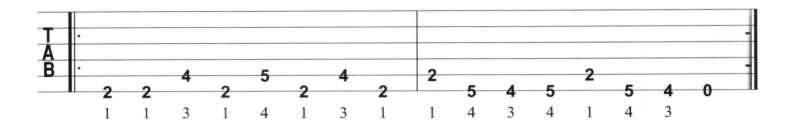

Rock Riffs 2

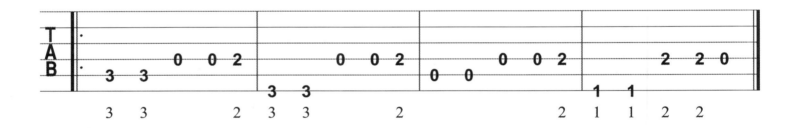

Rock Riffs 3

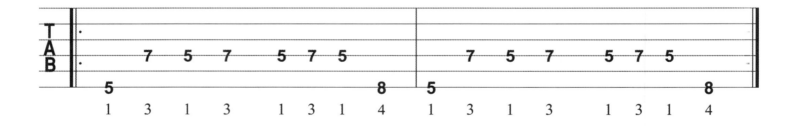

Rock Riffs 4

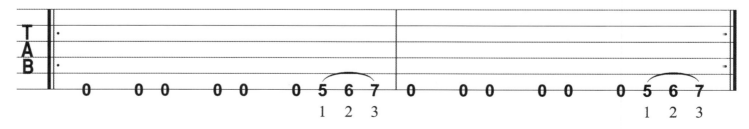

Hammer On & Pull Off Exercise

Hammer ons and pull offs are two more widely used lead techniques. On the staffs below, you'll see a slur connecting one tab number to the next. This indicates that only the first tab number is picked; the second note is not struck. The "H" above the slur indicates a hammer on, and the "P" indicates a pull off.

To play a hammer on, pick the first note and then push down the next note using just your left hand finger (without picking it). Play through the series of hammer ons in the first measure below to see how you can use these with the minor pentatonic scale.

Pull offs are the opposite of hammer ons. Pick the first note and pull or snap your finger off the string to the get the second note. Your first finger should already be in place, fretting the second note in advance.

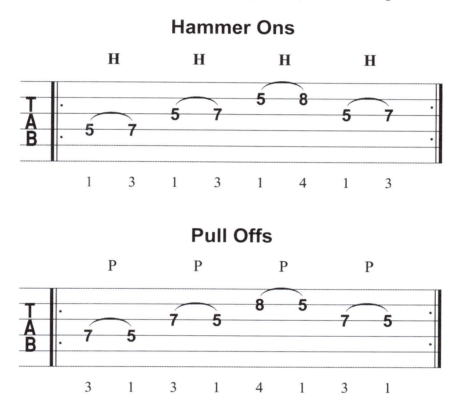

The following exercise contains hammer ons and pull offs in combination. The slurs encompass three notes, so only pick the first one. Hammer on for the second note, then pull off to the third note. At the very end of the second measure, you'll see a squiggly line above the last note. This line indicates a technique known as vibrato. While sustaining the note, shake your finger slightly and "dig in" to the note to slightly vibrate the pitch and give it more expression.

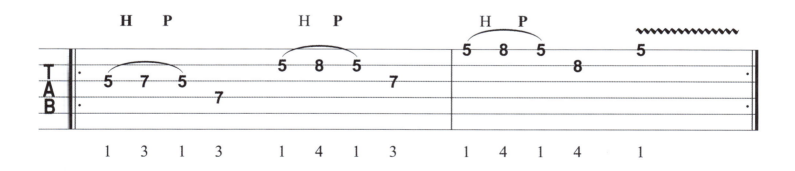

Full Blues Rhythm & Lead

Full Blues Rhythm

This standard blues rhythm is in A and uses a I - IV - V progression. The rhythm is similar to Blues Rhythm #1 from Lesson 10. Be sure to keep your first finger anchored at the 2nd fret while stretching with your fourth finger to fret the notes at the 5th fret. Practice along with the backing track to get the timing and the shuffle feel.

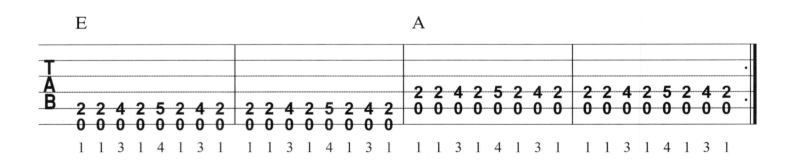

Here's an example of a solo that can be played over the shuffle blues rhythm you've just learned. This solo incorporates bends, hammer ons and pull offs in a variety of positions. The riff in the first measure is one of the most commonly used blues riffs; it can be heard in countless blues guitar solos. The last two measures contain a blues turnaround (a phrase used at the end of a 12-bar blues to bring you back around to the beginning of the progression). After you've got this solo down, try to create your own using all of the lead techniques and different positions of the A minor pentatonic scales.

Full Blues Lead

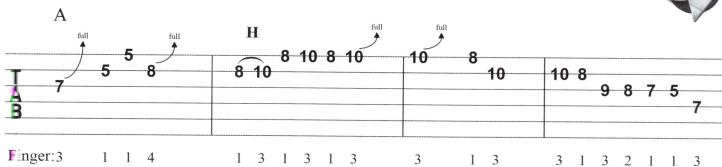
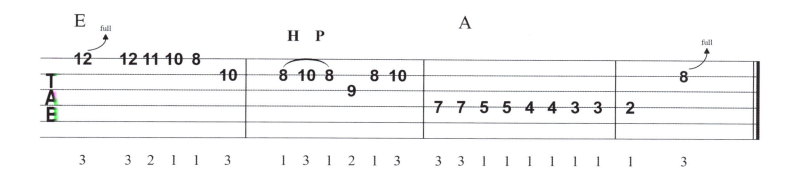

Quick Tip!

Play Slowly At First

When learning something new, don't start out trying to play it as fast as possible. Take things slowly at first; play slow enough so you don't keep making mistakes. Build your speed over time. A great tool for learning to build speed gradually is a metronome. This is a device that clicks at an adjustable rate that you set. A metronome allows you to gauge your progress each day. By playing along with the click, you learn to play in time with other instruments.

Single String Picking

This exercise is designed to strengthen your picking hand and increase coordination and control of the pick. Practice this exercise using any of the open strings; you don't need your left hand for this one at all. Use consistent, steady alternate picking and play continuously for about five minutes without stopping. You can practice this anytime, even while relaxing and watching TV.

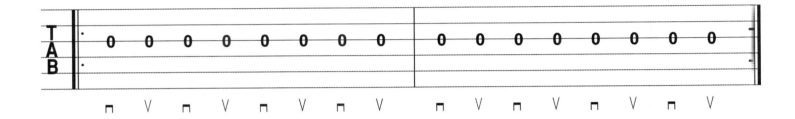

Minor Pentatonic Scales 4 - 5

Here are the last two positions of the A minor pentatonic scale. Practice and memorize both scale positions ascending and descending. You can also practice the scales using the Double Lead Pattern you learned earlier.

4th Position A Minor Pentatonic

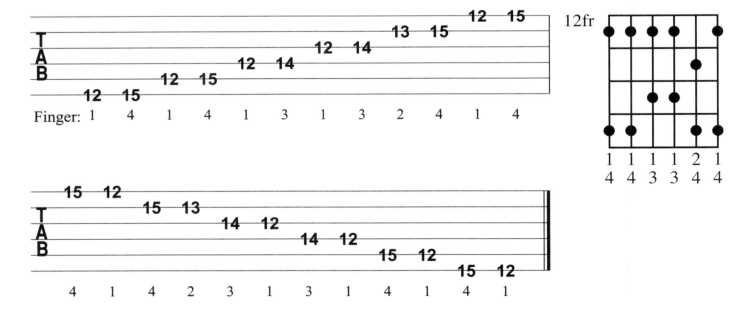

5th Position A Minor Pentatonic

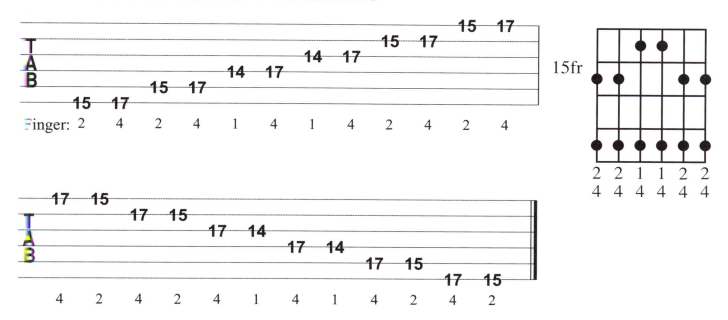

Minor Pentatonic Scale Fretboard Diagram

Once you have all five positions of the minor pentatonic scales mastered, you'll be able to play solos in any position on the neck. Remember that there are only five different name notes in the scale, and the different positions are just groupings of these same notes in different octaves and different places on the neck. The 4th and 5th positions from the previous page can be transpose done octave lower (shown below in the fretboard diagram). Notice how each position overlaps the next; the left side of one position is the right side of the next one and so on. Think of these scale positions as building blocks (like Legos). When soloing, you can move from position to position and play across the entire fretboard.

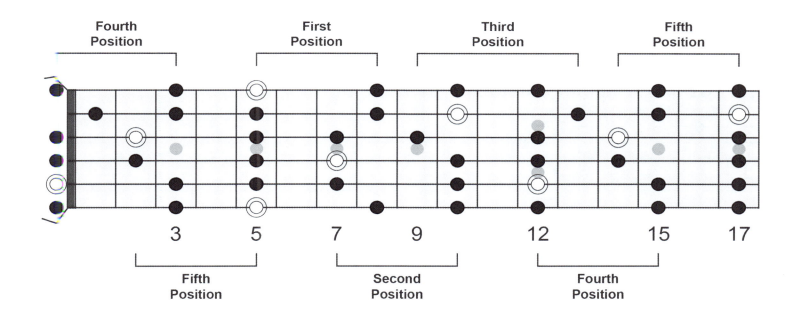

Triplet Lead Pattern

The following triplet lead pattern exercise uses the A minor pentatonic scale played in groups of three notes, or triplets. Count "one - two - three, one - two - three" out loud while you play through this exercise to get the triplet feel in your head. Memorizing and practicing lead patterns will help you get comfortable with playing the scales in the context of leads and solos. Practice this and all lead patterns along with a metronome to develop timing and control. The first example below uses the 1st position A minor pentatonic scale ascending.

1st Position A Minor Pentatonic - Ascending

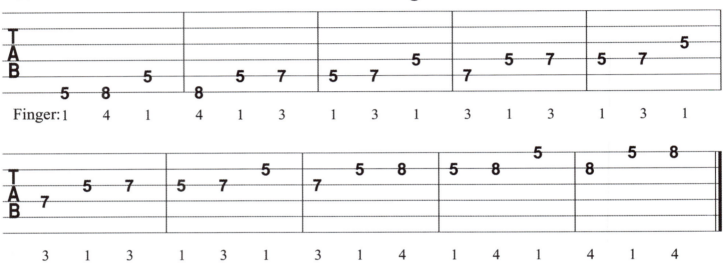

Now let's play the same pattern in reverse, back down the scale in triplets.

1st Position A Minor Pentatonic - Descending

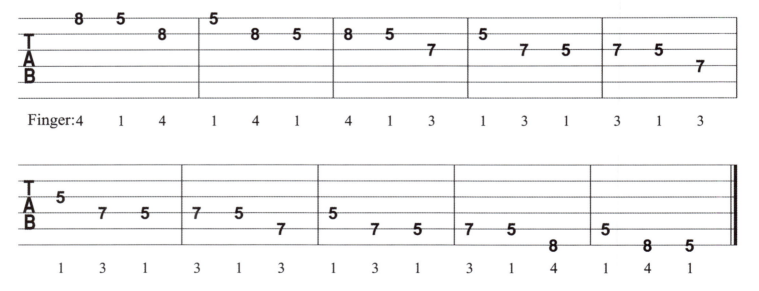

40

Practice every position of the A minor pentatonic scale using the triplet lead pattern and alternate picking. The 2nd position ascending and descending triplet patterns are shown below.

2nd Position A Minor Pentatonic

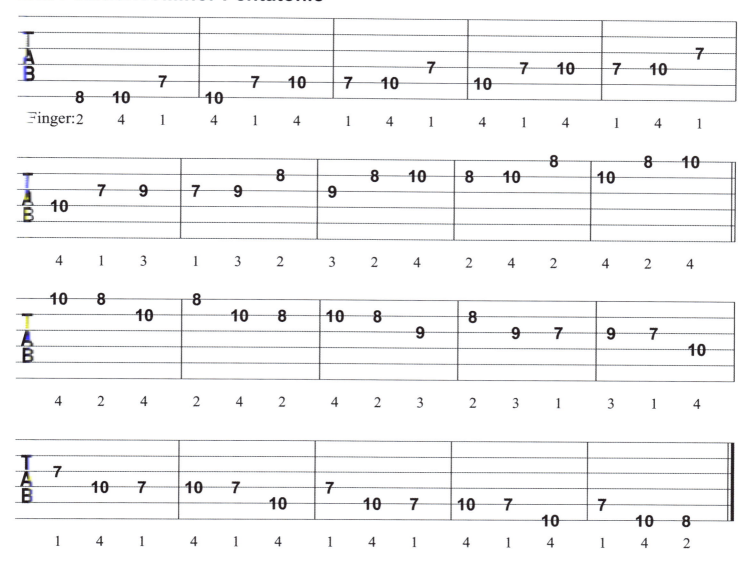

Quick Tip!

Test Your Memory

The easiest way to memorize a piece is through repetition. The more you repeat each part, the easier it will be to hear in your head. You may find it easier to memorize something by breaking it into small sections. Be sure to have the first few bits down before moving on and memorization should begin to happen naturally.

Rock Rhythm & Lead

For the last section of this program we'll use a complete rock rhythm and show you how to solo over it. First learn the rhythm part and play it along with the backing track. This is a rhythm based on bar chords in the key of A minor.

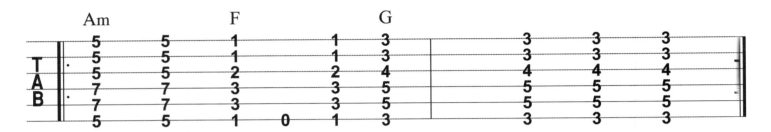

The following guitar solo incorporates all of the lead techniques and covers several positions of the minor pentatonic scale. After you've got this lead down, get creative and try improvising along with the backing track in every position of the A minor pentatonic, using bends, hammer ons and pull offs. You should now have a solid foundation for playing your own rock and blues solos.

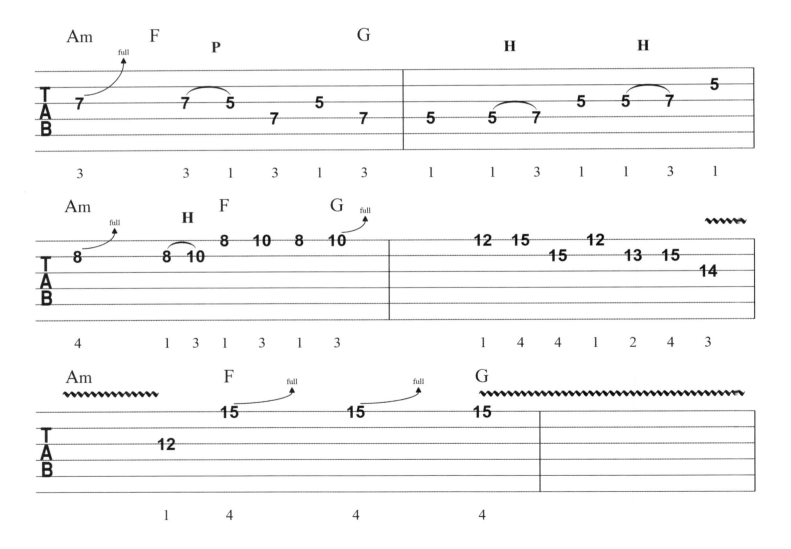

42

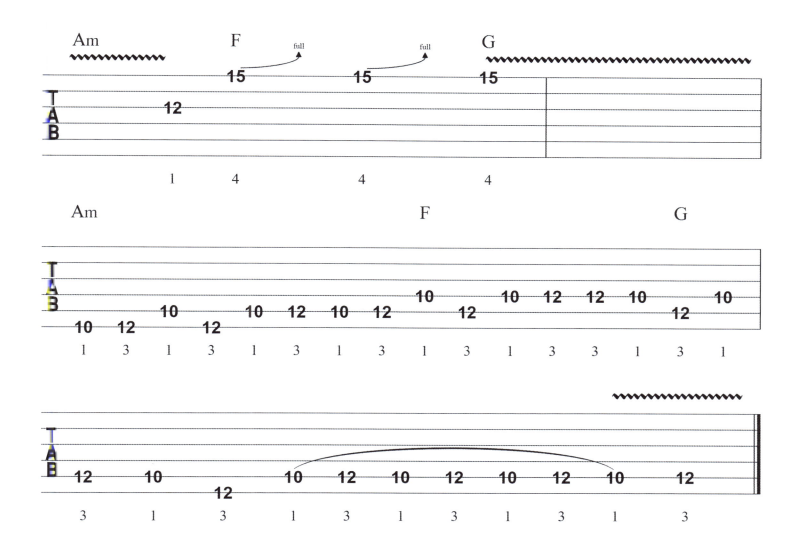

Quick Tip!

Learn Gradually & Have Realistic Goals

Don't try to play a lot of things you aren't ready for. Be realistic about your capabilities as a beginner and learn gradually. If you progress at a steady, methodical rate, your technique and control of the guitar will become solid as you advance. Strive to master each new technique, chord or scale before moving on to something else. Attempting things that you're not quite ready for can discourage you instead of inspire you to play.

Review Quiz 1

1) The names of the open strings, from lowest to highest pitched, are:
A. B-E-G-A-D-E
B. A-G-E-B-E-D
C. E-A-D-G-B-E
D. A-B-C-D-E-F

2) A bar is executed by
A. Placing one finger flat across more than one string
B. Playing all the notes of a chord separately
C. Holding the guitar upside down
D. Holding the pick between your index finger and thumb

3) A series of chords played in a specified rhythm and order is called a
A. Song
B. Chord diagram
C. Chord progression
D. Symphony

4) Quarter notes are held for
A. One quarter of a beat
B. Four beats
C. One beat
D. A quarter of a second

5) Consistent down-up-down-up picking is called
A. Alternative picking
B. Up and down picking
C. Alternate picking
D. Back and forth picking

6) The two major open chords that require you to bar more than one note are
A. C and G
B. A and F
C. D and E
D. G and B

7) The six lines of the tablature staff represent
A. Six different chords
B. The six strings of the guitar
C. The first six frets on the guitar
D. Nothing

8) If two or more numbers are stacked together on the tablature staff, those notes should be
A. Ignored
B. Played one at a time
C. Played backwards
D. Played together

9) 12-bar blues is
A. A blues progression consisting of 12 measures of repeated music
B. 12 minutes long
C. A standard heavy metal progression
D. Always in the key of G

10) Most blues songs are played using
A. Minor chords
B. A shuffle feel
C. All major chords
D. A metronome

11) Minor pentatonic scales contain
A. Five different notes
B. Only minor notes
C. One beat
D. Seven different notes

12) Minor chords have
A. Triplets
B. Two notes
C. A sad or melancholy sound
D. A happy, bright sound

13) Bar chords are
A. Moveable chords
B. Easy to play
C. Open string chords
D. Only used in jazz

14) Two frequently used lead techniques are
A. Tuning and strumming
B. Bar chords and open chords
C. Hammer ons and pull offs
D. Eighth notes and quarter notes

15) A repeated theme made up of single notes is
A. Repetitive
B. Boring
C. A riff
D. A pentatonic scale

16) The slight shaking of a sustained note is
A. A hammer on
B. Vibrato
C. A bend
D. A shuffle

Answers on Page 96

Guitar Solo

This solo is an inspirational piece that contains many of the scales and techniques that are taught in my Learn Rock Guitar Beginner, Intermediate, and Advanced programs. When trying to learn a challenging piece you should break it down into small sections, mastering each before moving to the next. I hope you enjoy your musical journey.
- John McCarthy

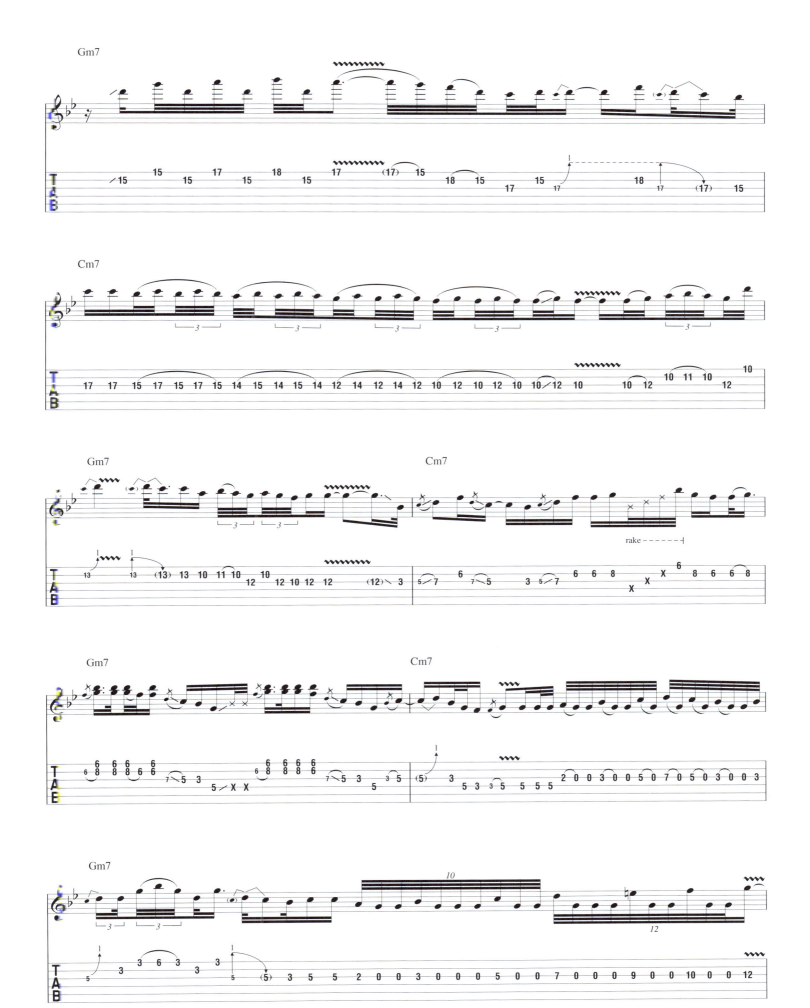

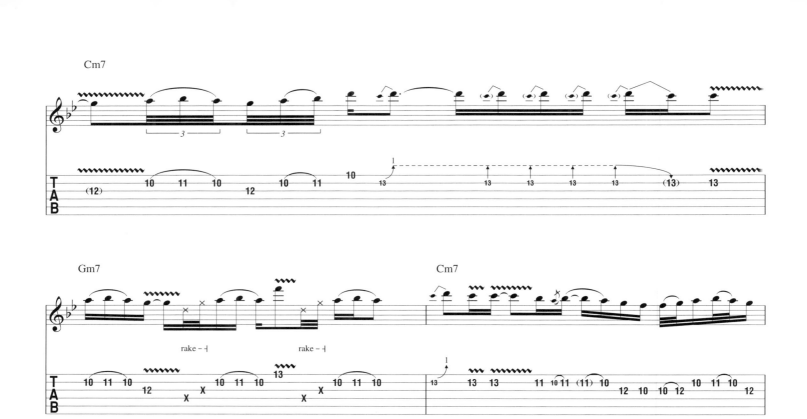
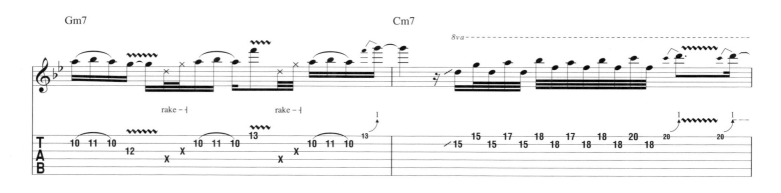
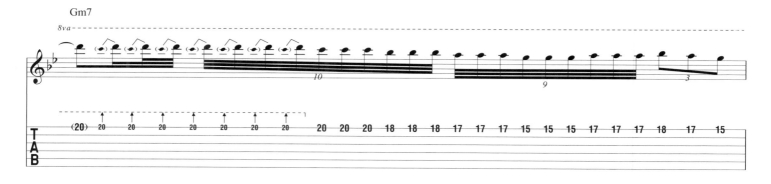
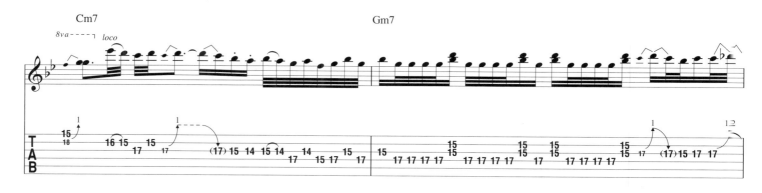

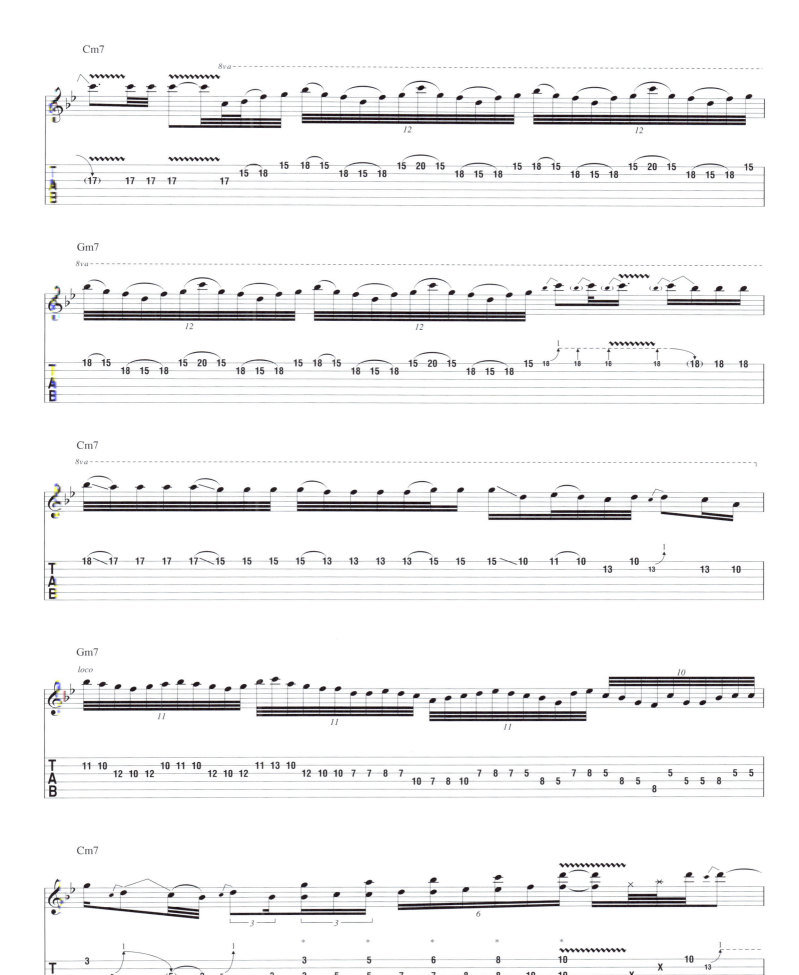

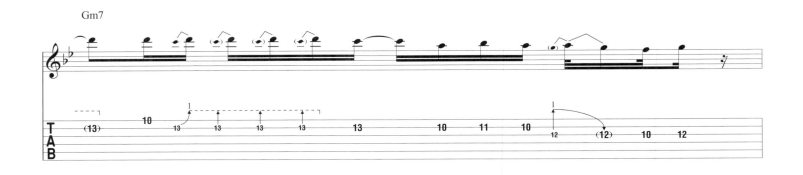
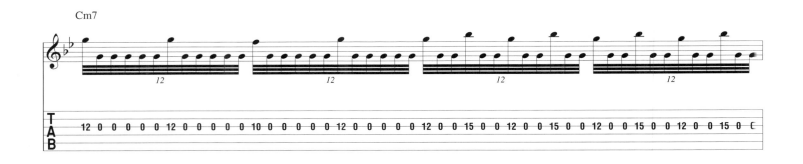
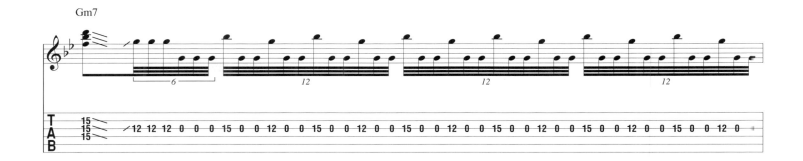
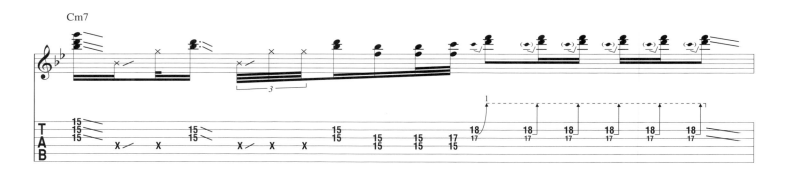
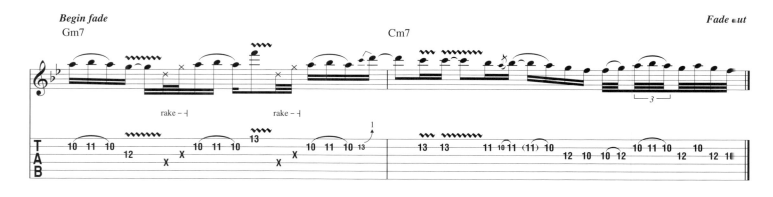

Review Open Chords

Major Open Chords

A

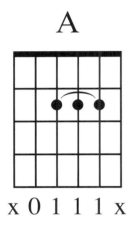

x 0 1 1 1 x

B

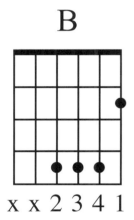

x x 2 3 4 1

C

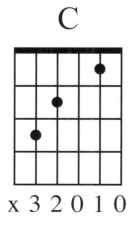

x 3 2 0 1 0

D

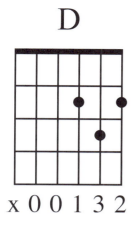

x 0 0 1 3 2

E

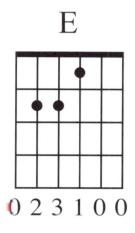

0 2 3 1 0 0

F

x x 3 2 1 1

G

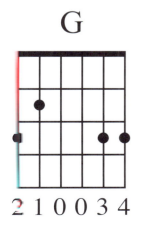

2 1 0 0 3 4

Minor Open Chords

Am

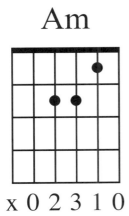

x 0 2 3 1 0

Bm

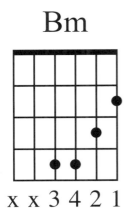

x x 3 4 2 1

Cm

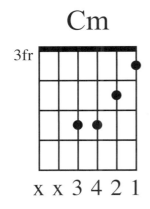

3fr

x x 3 4 2 1

Dm

x 0 0 2 3 1

Em

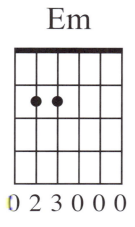
0 2 3 0 0 0

Fm

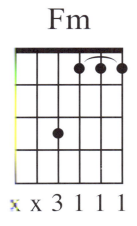
x x 3 1 1 1

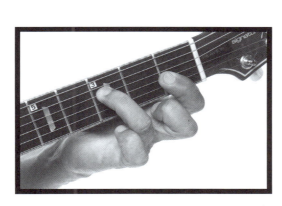

Gm

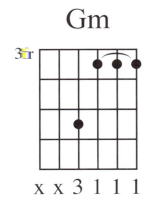
x x 3 1 1 1

Review Pentatonic Scales

Minor pentatonic scales are the most commonly used scales for playing rock and blues solos. The pentatonic scale is a five note scale, or an abbreviated version of the full natural minor scale. The word "pentatonic" comes from the greek words, "penta" (five) and "tonic" (the keynote). The following chart shows the notes in the A natural minor scale and the A minor pentatonic scale. The minor pentatonic is comprised of the 1st, 3rd, 4th, 5th and 7th steps of the natural minor scale. The first step (or note) of a scale is referred to as the root note. The root note is the note that gives a scale or chord its letter name. The root note of the A natural minor scale and the A minor pentatonic scale is the note A.

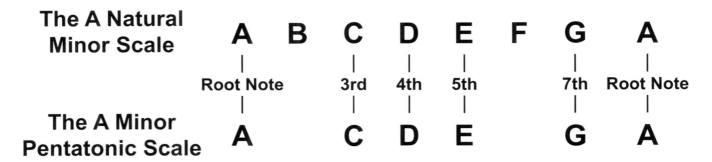

Memorize and practice this scale; it's the one you'll use most often for playing melodies and leads. There are five different positions of this scale, each beginning on a different note of the scale. All five positions are shown here in tab. To the right of each tab staff is a scale diagram. Suggested fingerings are shown beneath the tab staffs and scale diagrams, and the root notes(all of the A's) have been circled for your reference.

1st Position A Minor Pentatonic

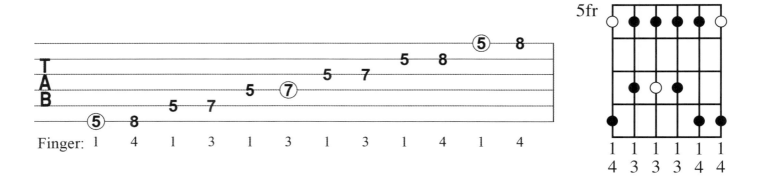

2nd Position A Minor Pentatonic

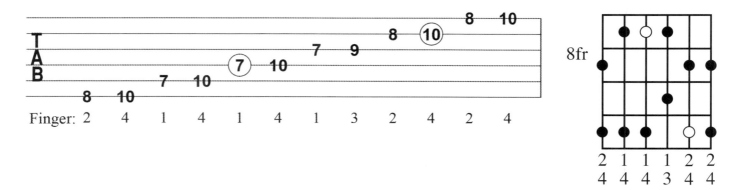

3rd Position A Minor Pentatonic

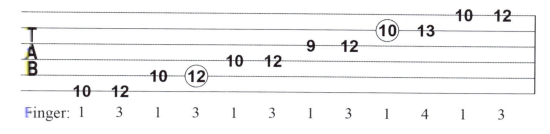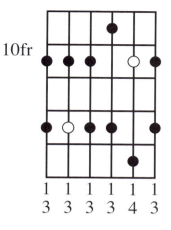

4th Position A Minor Pentatonic

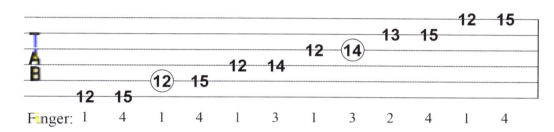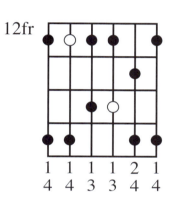

5th Position A Minor Pentatonic

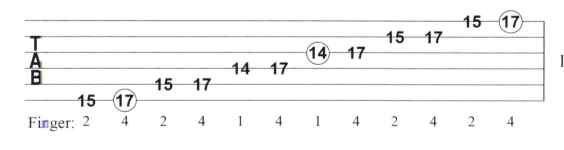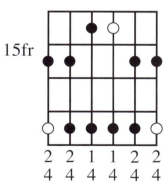

Minor Pentatonic Scale Fretboard Diagram

Once you have all five positions of the minor pentatonic scales mastered, you'll be able to play solos in any position on the neck. Remember that there are only five different name notes in the scale, and the different positions are just groupings of these same notes in different octaves and different places on the neck. The 4th and 5th positions from the previous page can be transposed one octave lower (shown below in the fretboard diagram). Notice how each position overlaps the next; the left side of one position is the right side of the next one and so on. Think of these scale positions as building blocks (like Legos). When soloing, you can move from position to position and play across the entire fretboard. Memorize where all of the circled root notes are and think of them as your home base, or tonal center.

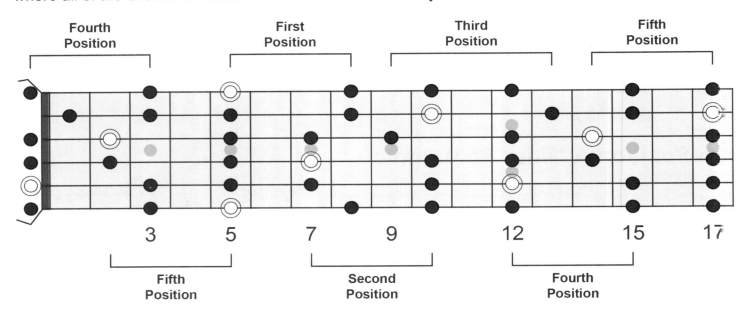

Lead Patterns

The following examples are standard lead pattern exercises, designed to help you build coordination and learn how to begin using the minor pentatonics for playing leads. Use alternate picking and the metronome to start out slowly and get the rhythm. Memorize the patterns and gradually speed up the tempo. Before you know it, you'll be playing blazing rock and blues guitar solos.

1st Position Minor Pentatonic

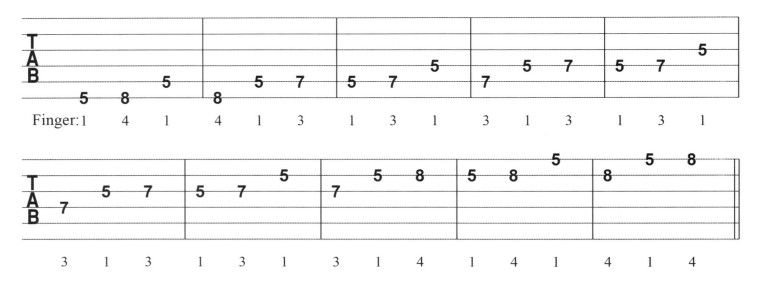

58

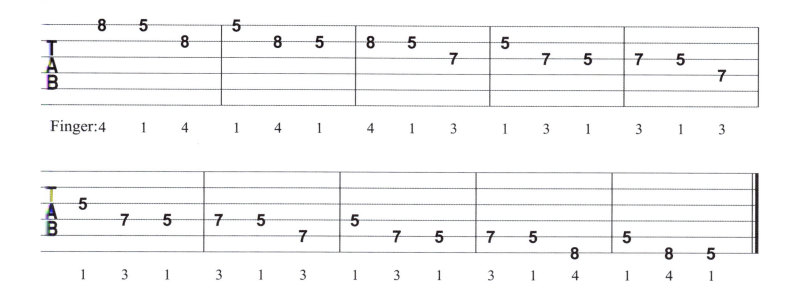

2nd Position Minor Pentatonic

Practice every position of the A minor pentatonic scale using the triplet lead pattern and alternate picking. The 2nd position ascending and descending triplet patterns are shown below. You can find more examples of lead patterns on the Lesson Support Site.

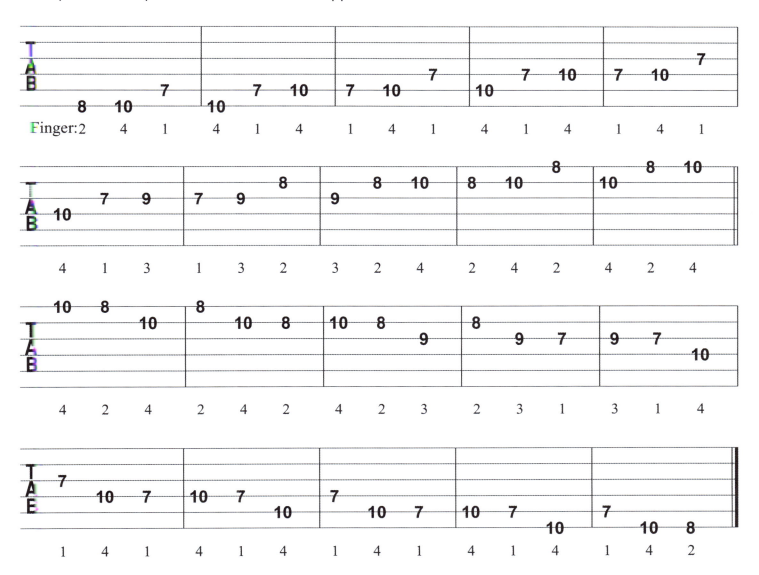

Hammer On & Pull Off Lead Pattern (1st Position)

The next lead pattern is a little more complex and uses a three note combination hammer on and pull off within each measure. Pick only the first note of each hammer on and pull off phrase, indicated by a slur above the tab staff. For each of these phrases, fret and hold the first note, then hammer on to the second note and pull off back to the original note in one smooth motion. The fingering underneath the staff shows you which left hand fingers to use for each hammer on and pull off combination. The first two tab staffs show the pattern ascending through the 1st position of the A minor pentatonic scale. The next two staffs descend through the same position, using a slightly different rhythm and phrasing. As before, start out practicing slowly along with a metronome and build up speed gradually. Once you've got it down, try to experiment with different patterns and rhythms and come up with some of your own ideas.

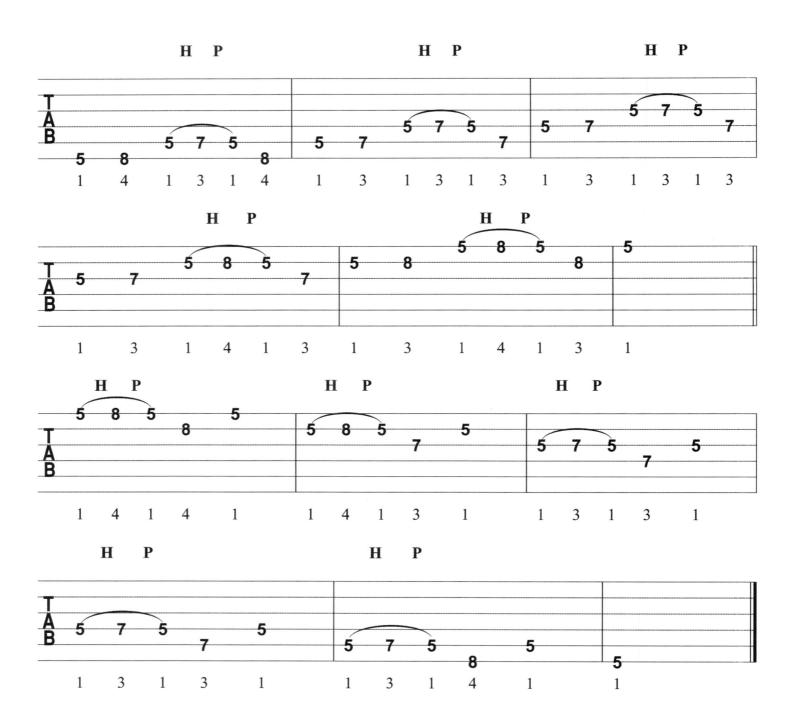

60

Hammer On & Pull Off Lead Pattern (2nd Position)

Here's the same hammer on & pull off pattern shown in the 2nd position. This one may seem slightly harder to play because the frets are farther apart in the 2nd position. Playing this pattern in all five positions will give you a great workout and help build up endurance in your left hand.

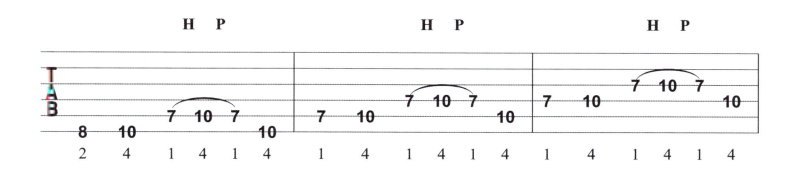

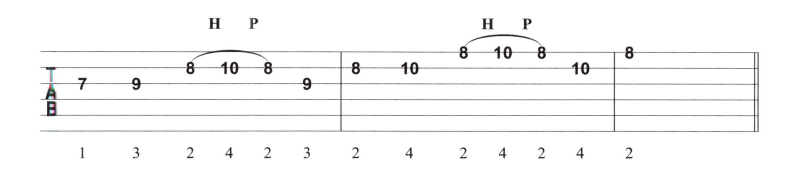

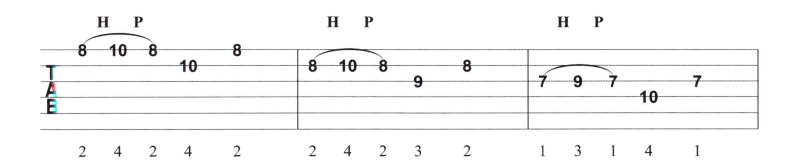

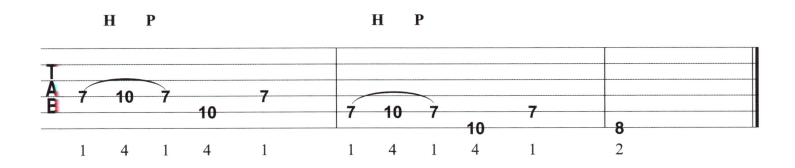

Bending Exercise

The following three riffs utilize different bending techniques in the context of a lead. Each riff uses the A minor pentatonic scale in a different position. These are just a few examples of how to use bending techniques in the context of scales and leads using different left hand fingers. The first riff is played in the 1st position of the scale and contains a few examples of the bend and release technique. To bend and release, bend the note up to the correct pitch, then release the bend and bring the note back to its original pitch without picking the string again. When performing fourth finger bends, use all of your other left hand fingers behind the fretted note to help push up and control the pitch of the bend.

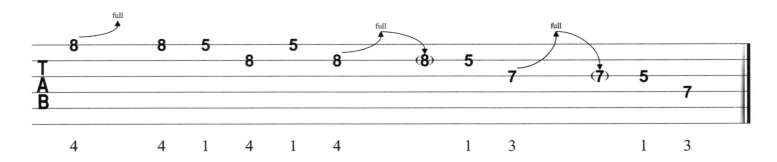

This next riff is played in the 2nd position and contains a first finger bend. This bend is slightly more difficult because you need to push up on the string using only one finger. Listen to the pitch of the bend to make sure you're pushing the string up far enough and the resulting note doesn't fall flat.

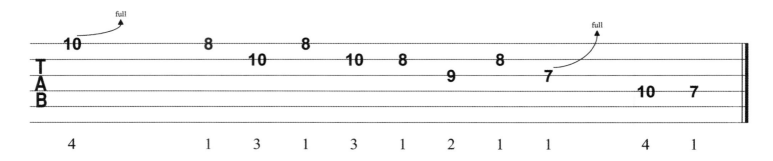

The third riff is played in the 4th position at the 12th fret and contains a second finger bend. The squiggly line at the end of this riff is an example of vibrato. Vibrato is the small, fast shaking of a note. While sustaining the note, shake your finger slightly and "dig in" to the note to slightly vibrate the pitch and give it more expression. Vibrato can also be applied while bending a note.

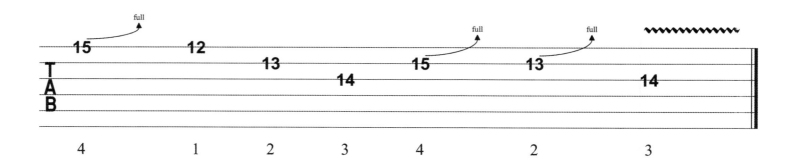

Bar Chords

Let's begin this section by expanding your chord vocabulary. The following full bar chords contain no open strings, so they are moveable chords; you can transpose them to any fret. After mastering these chords, you'll be able to play in any key and position on the guitar.

6th String Bar Chords

The first chord is F major. This chord is especially difficult to play because you need to bar across all six strings with your first finger, then add the other three notes as well. Pick out each note individually to make sure the chord sounds clean.

1 3 4 2 1 1

Notice that the lowest note of the chord is F, the root note. Using the musical alphabet, you can move bar chords up the neck and change them to any chord in the scale. Use the following chart to find any chord along the 6th string by moving the F chord. The name of the chord will change depending on which fret you move the chord to.

Name -	F	F#	G	G#	A	A#	B	C	C#	D	D#	E
Fret -	1	2	3	4	5	6	7	8	9	10	11	12

Once you've learned the F bar chord, simply lift your second finger and you'll have the Fm bar chord. The F7 (also called the F dominant seventh) bar chord is only slightly different from the F as well; just reposition your fourth finger and you've got it. Dominant seventh chords are often used in blues as substitutes for major chords.

1 3 4 1 1 1

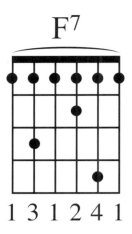

F^7

1 3 1 2 4 1

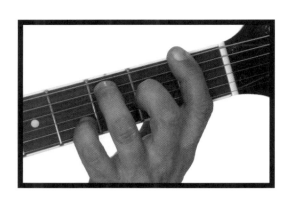

5th String Bar Chords

The Bb major bar chord is played at the 1st fret with the root note on the 5th string. This chord has a third finger bar. Make sure the 1st and 6th strings are muted and not strummed. Use the chart below to transpose this chord to any other fret along the 5th string.

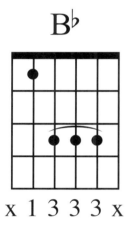

$B^\flat$

x 1 3 3 3 x

Name -	Bb	B	C	C#	D	D#	E	F	F#	G	G#	A
Fret -	1	2	3	4	5	6	7	8	9	10	11	12

The Bbm and Bb7 bar chords are played using a first finger bar. Once you have them mastered, try transposing both chords to other frets using the 5th string chart on the previous page.

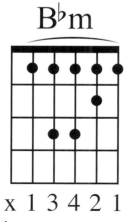

$B^\flat m$

x 1 3 4 2 1

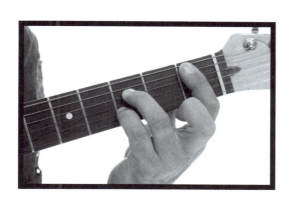

Rhythms To Play Scales & Patterns Over
Open Chord Rhythm & Lead

This chord progression combines both major and minor chords in the key of A minor. The four chords used in the progression are shown in order using chord diagrams below. Use the alternate fingering for the Em chord (with your first and second fingers) to make changing from chord to chord easier. Notice how similar the fingerings are between the Am and C chords; simply move your third finger and leave your other fingers stationary. Play along with the backing track and practice changing chords cleanly and in time. Use the strumming pattern indicated by the symbols above the tab staff.

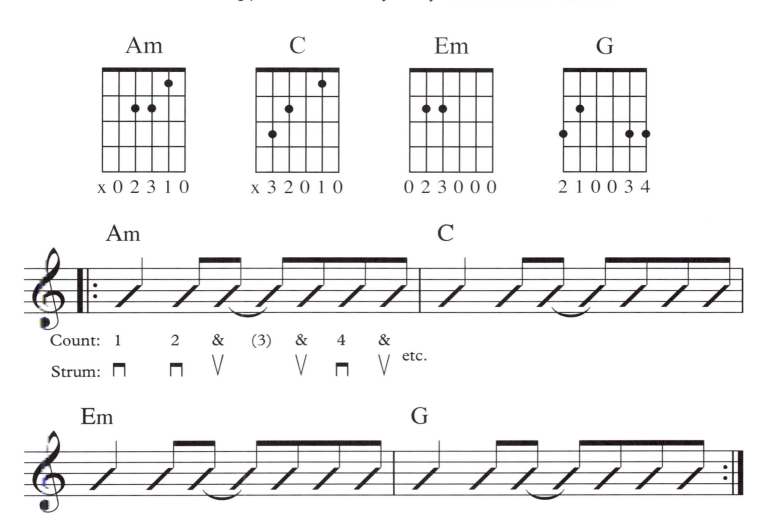

Once you've got the rhythm down, you can practice playing lead patterns and scales along with the backing track. You can use all five positions of the A minor pentatonic scale to improvise and try changing from position to position cleanly and in time. Start out by playing the triplet lead pattern or the hammer on and pull off pattern, then mix it up and experiment to come up with your own ideas. The following example lead can be played over the Open Chord Rhythm. The chord symbols have been included above the staff as a reference. Play through this example to get some ideas, then make up your own leads.

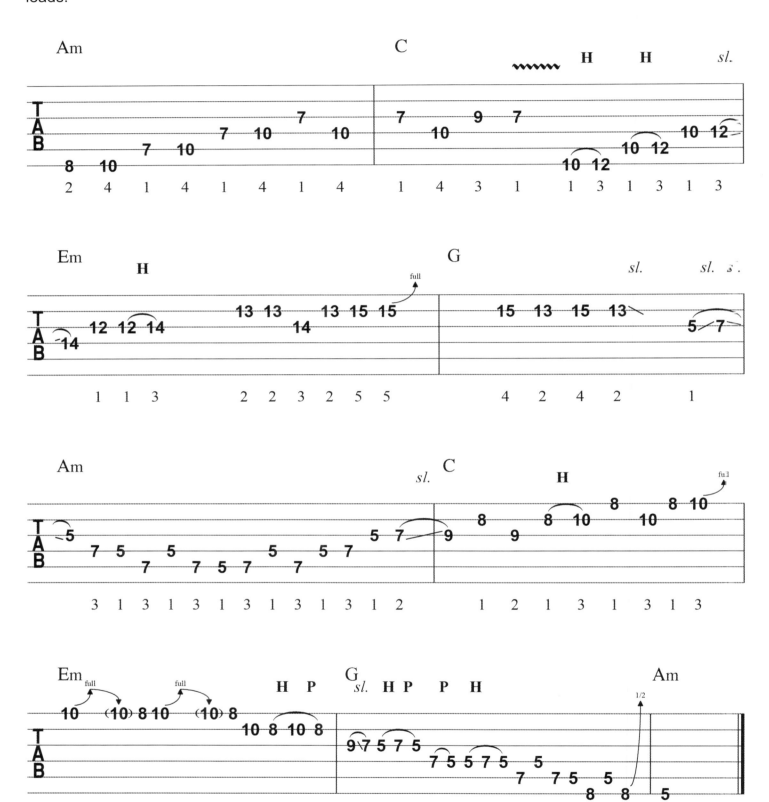

Workout Section

The following workout section contains a series of exclusive Rock House finger exercises designed to strengthen specific areas of your playing technique. All of these exercises should be practiced along with a metronome. Start out slowly and build speed gradually. Use alternate picking when required and always be sure to use proper fret hand technique.

The Killer!!

This exercise is designed to work on your left hand coordination. Use consistent alternate picking throughout. Play through the first measure slowly until you memorize the pattern. Notice that all four fingers of the left hand are used in succession. For each consecutive measure,

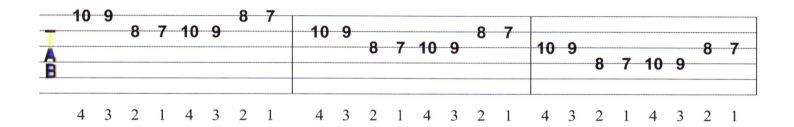

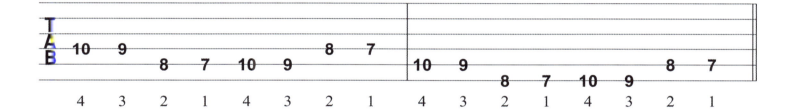

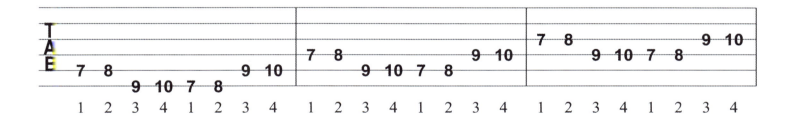

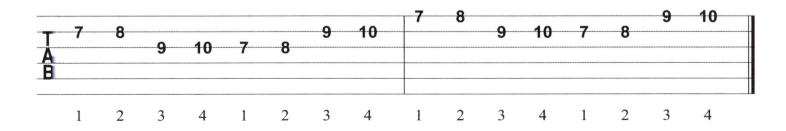

Hammer Rolls

This exercise will help to strengthen the hammer on and pull off techniques. The fingering and fret numbers are the same on each string, and the pattern moves up in groups of three strings for each measure. Play each group of three notes using a smooth triplet feel, picking the first note and hammering on for the next two notes. The second tab staff shows the example in reverse, this time using pull offs and moving down in groups of three strings.

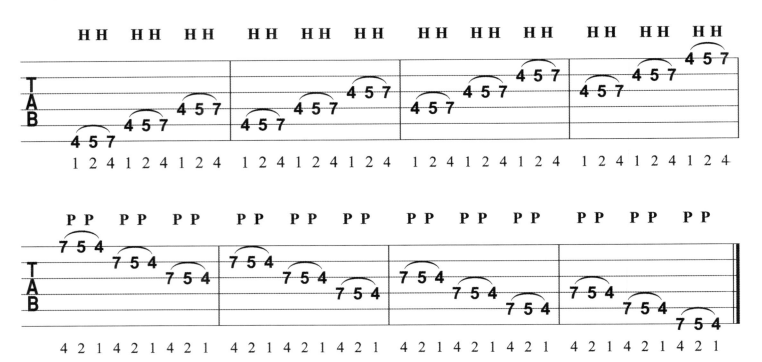

Speed Pick

The Speed Pick exercise is designed to strengthen your picking hand and increase coordination and control of the pick. Practice this exercise using all open strings; you don't need your left hand for this one at all. Follow the picking symbols to get the pattern correct. Repeat each measure for 30 seconds, then repeat the entire exercise for a full five minutes every day. You can practice this anytime, even while relaxing and watching TV.

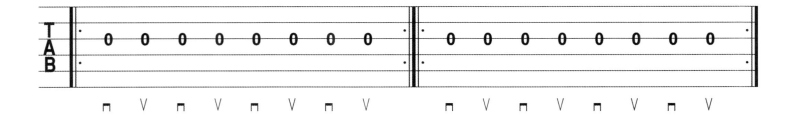

The Finger Crusher

The finger crusher is a left hand workout that will make your fingers stronger and faster. Each section of the exercise starts with a two string pattern from the minor pentatonic scale. Play it four times in position, then move the pattern chromatically (one fret at a time) up the neck to the 12th fret and chromatically back down to where you started at the 5th fret. Your hand will probably get sore and tired before you're even halfway through the exercise, but that just means you're doing it right and getting a great workout. Try to keep time with the metronome and make it your goal to get through the entire exercise without stopping.

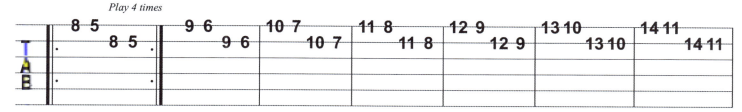

Finger: 4 1 4 1 etc.

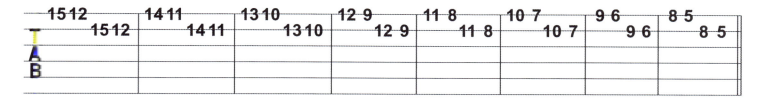

4 1 3 1 etc.

Finger: 3 1 3 1 etc.

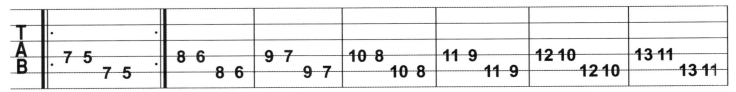

Play 4 times

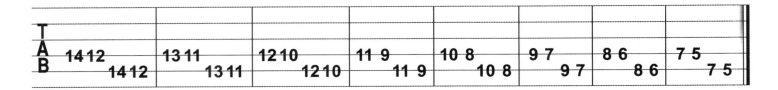

3 1 3 1   etc.

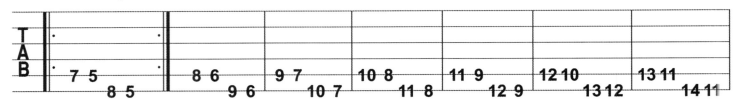

Play 4 times

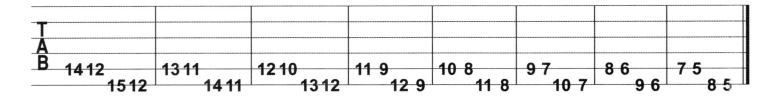

Finger: 3 1 4 1   etc.

Practice Tips

To ensure constant progress and high motivation you have to develop practice habits that will keep you interested and challenged. Here are a few tips:

Practice Consistently - You need to give your fingers a chance to gain muscle memory. Practice every day even if it is for a short amount of time, be consistent.

Practice Area - Have a practice spot set up so you can have privacy to focus on your playing. It is a great idea to have a music stand to help position your music so you can sit comfortably.

Practice Schedule - Set a scheduled practice time each day and make this a routine. Other times in the day you can play for fun and jam a little.

One Hand Rolls

Here's an exercise designed to strengthen your left hand using a series of hammer ons and pull offs. Pick the very first note of the exercise, then all of the notes should be produced by the left hand only; don't use the pick at all for the rest of the notes. Your right hand can be used to mute the other strings.

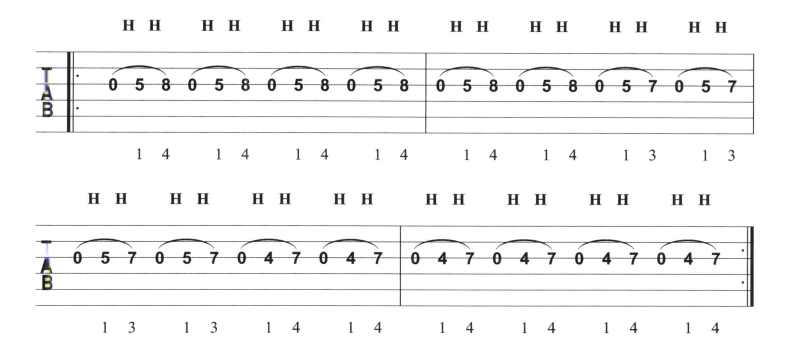

Using the Metronome to Practice

As you progress as a guitarist you can use the metronome in your daily practice to help keep a steady rhythm and gauge your progress. Here are a few metronome practice tips that will help you use this tool effectively.

1. When starting to learn a new song set the metronome at a slow tempo where you can play the entire piece through without making mistakes.

2. Gradually build your speed by increasing the BPM (beats per minute) on the metronome a few numbers each day.

3. As you play with the metronome try not to focus on it too much. Sense the feel of the click and concentrate on the song you are playing.

Blues Rhythm & Lead

This is a standard I - IV - V blues progression in the key of E. The chords are all basic two note chords. Use all down picking and play the rhythm using a shuffle feel. Once you've got it memorized play along with the bass and drum backing track to get the shuffle feel mastered.

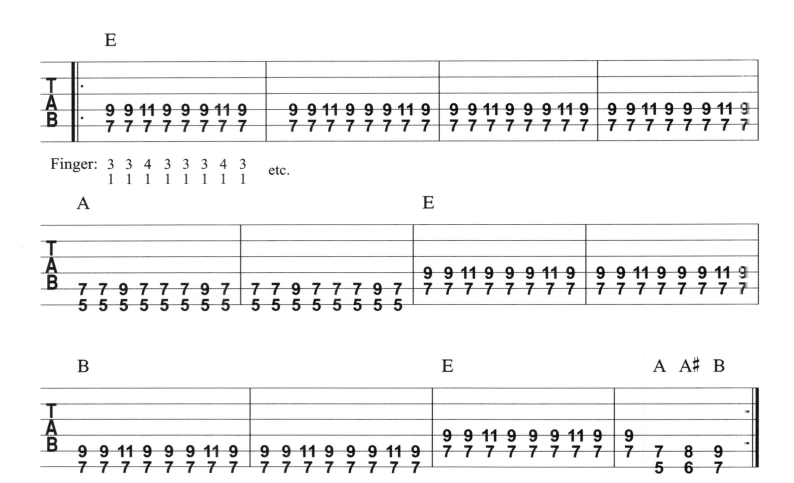

You can play the following lead over the Blues Rhythm for an example of how to solo using the pentatonic scales in E. All of the basic lead techniques we've covered so far are represented here. Remember to use a shuffle feel when playing blues solos and riffs.

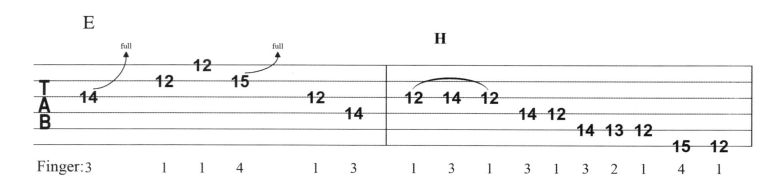

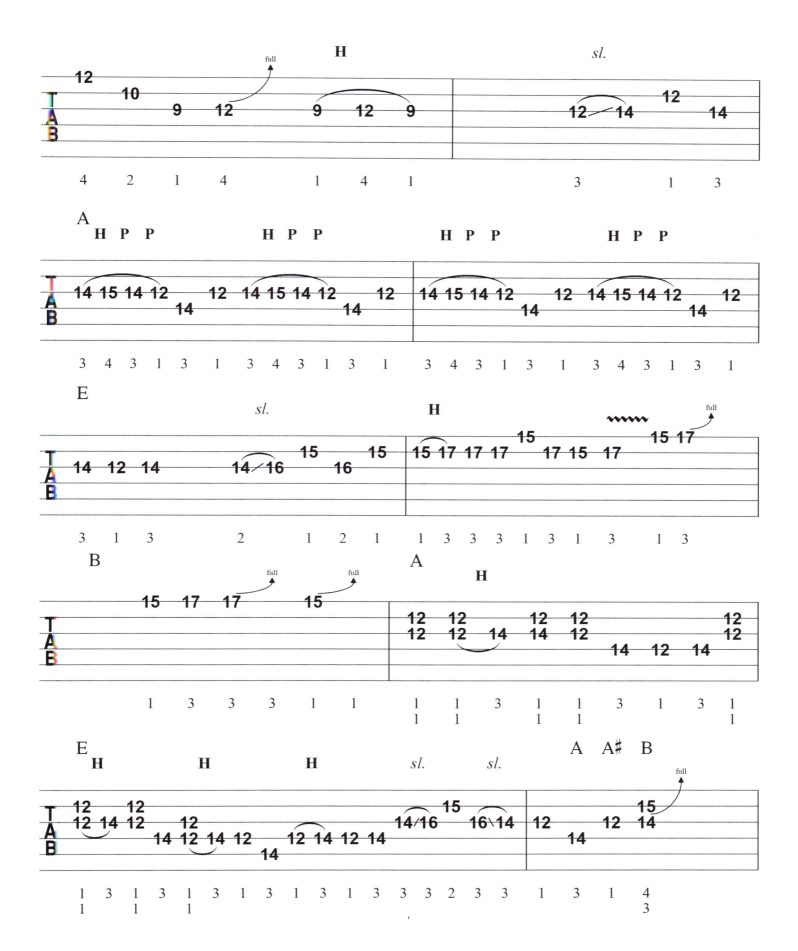

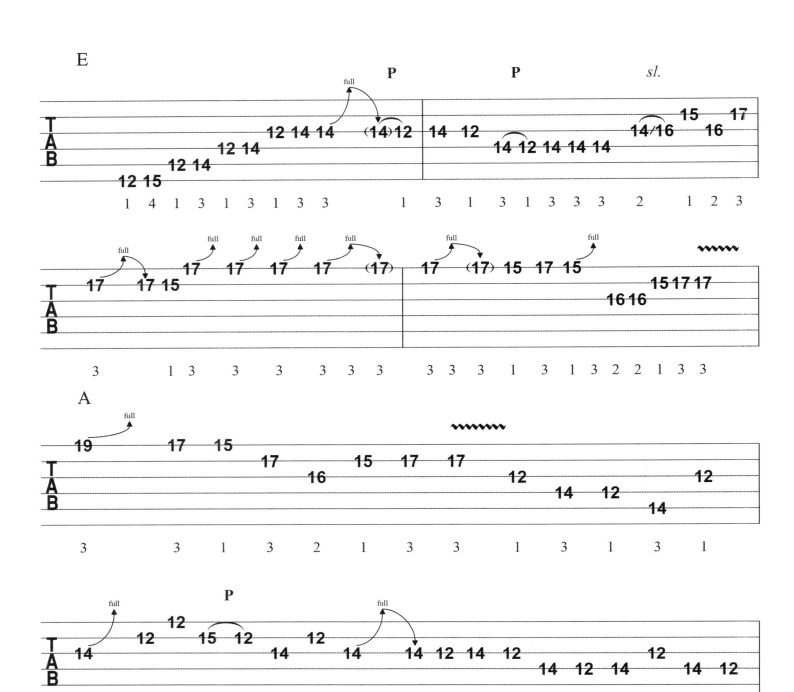

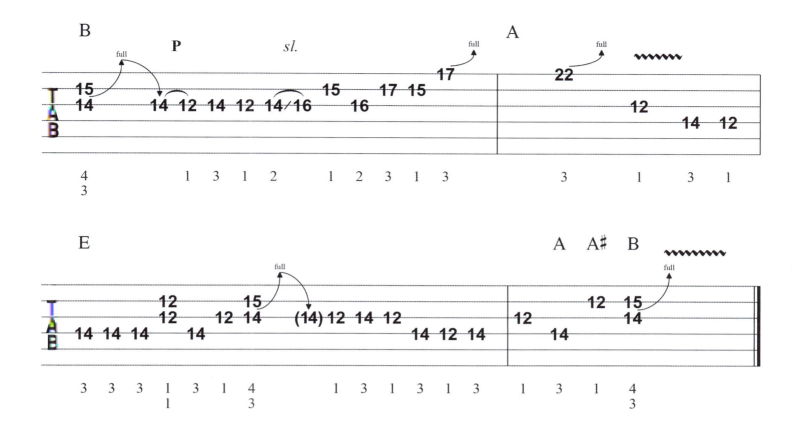

Vibrato

Vibrato is a rapid, slight variation in a notes pitch producing a stronger or richer tone. This is achieved on the guitar by shaking your hand in very small rapid movements after you pick a note. This creates a pulsating effect similar to a singer's vibrato. Make sure not to bend the notes pitch. Vibrato is designated by a squiggly line above a note. Play the two notes to the right and apply the vibrato technique.

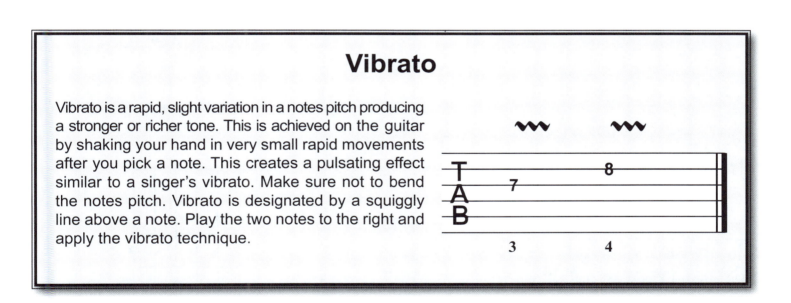

Blues Scales

The blues scale is a slight variation of the minor pentatonic scale. It contains one extra note between the 4th and 5th steps of the scale, called a passing tone. This particular passing tone is the flatted fifth of the scale, also known as the blues tri-tone. Using the blues tri-tone adds color and character to solos and riffs. This note is a chromatic passing tone because it passes from the 4th to the 5th steps of the scale in chromatic half steps. Passing tones are used to connect from note to note within a phrase and are generally not held for long durations.

The following five scale positions of the E blues scale are the same as the E minor pentatonic scale with the addition of the blues tri-tone. The Xs in the scale diagrams to the right indicate where the blues tri-tones are played. Practice and memorize the E blues scale positions; we'll be using these scales to play solos in many of the following sections.

1st Position A Blues Scale

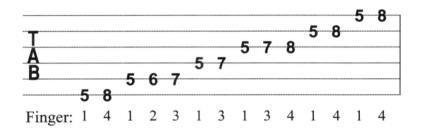
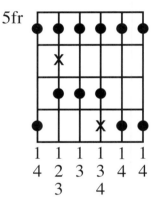

2nd Position A Blues Scale

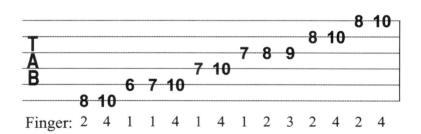
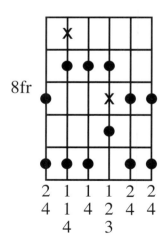

3rd Position A Blues Scale

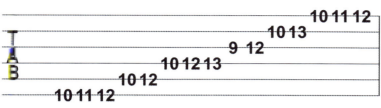
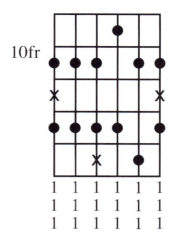

4th Position A Blues Scale

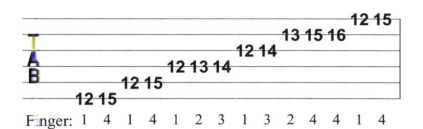
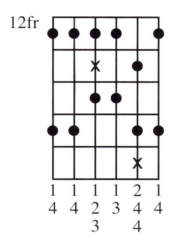

5th Position A Blues Scale

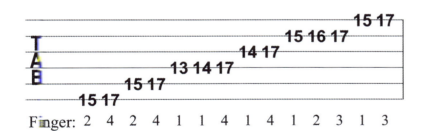
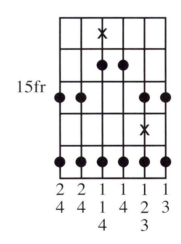

A Blues Scale Fretboard Diagram

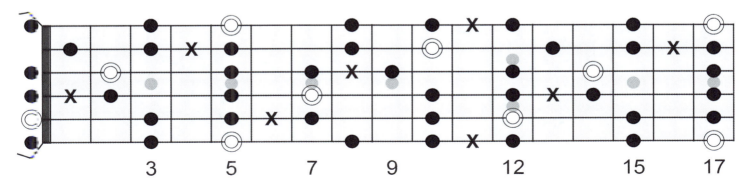

Arpeggios

An arpeggio is defined as the notes of a chord played separately. Major and minor arpeggios contain three different name notes: the root note (which is the same note as the arpeggio or chord's letter name), the third (which is the third scale step and letter name up from the root note), and the fifth (the fifth scale step and letter name up from the root note). Full major and minor chords on the guitar are actually groups of root notes, thirds and fifths in different octaves that your hand can reach within that position. Once you know the theory behind which individual notes belong in the chord and where they are on the fretboard, you can create your own chords. More information on arpeggio and chord theory can be found at www.rockhousemethod.com and in the Learn Rock Guitar Advanced program.

Major Arpeggio

The following examples are two octave A major arpeggios. In the first example, follow the picking symbols and use normal, consistent alternate picking.

Alternate Picking

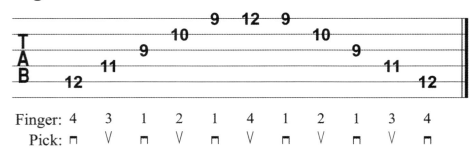

Now try the same A major arpeggio using the sweep picking technique. Sweep picking is performed by dragging the pick across the strings in one smooth, flowing motion. In the example below, sweep downward with the pick across the ascending part of the arpeggio. Play the three notes on the 1st string using a combination hammer on and pull off and then sweep back up across the strings with the pick using the same smooth motion. Sweep picking is a very useful technique for playing fast arpeggio runs. The downward sweep picking motion is also referred to as *raking*. This technique may be indicated in music and tablature using the word "rake" followed by a dashed line.

Sweep Picking

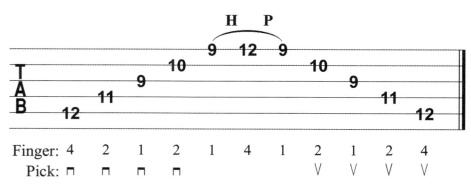

Minor Arpeggio

Here are the A minor arpeggios using alternate picking and sweep picking. Just like with full chords, major arpeggios have a happy or bright tone, while minor arpeggios have a sad or melancholy tone.

Alternate Picking

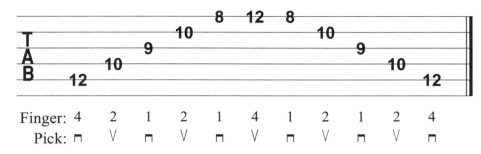

Sweep Picking

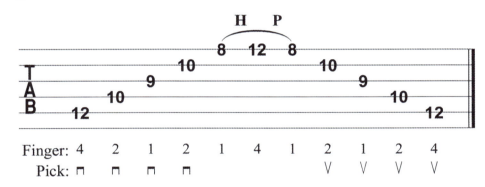

Notice there is only a small difference between the major and minor arpeggios. All of the thirds in the minor arpeggios are one fret (or one half step) lower than the thirds in the major arpeggio. This slight difference is what makes a chord or an arpeggio either major or minor. These notes are also referred to as *major thirds* or *minor thirds*.

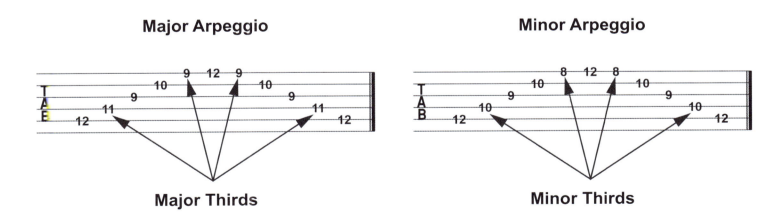

79

Rock Rhythm & Melodic Lead
Rock Rhythm

This is a simple rock rhythm that you can play along with the bass and drum backing track (also available on the Lesson Support Site). Follow the count below the tab staff the get the rhythm. When you've got it down, proceed to the following page for a melodic riff that you can play over this progression.

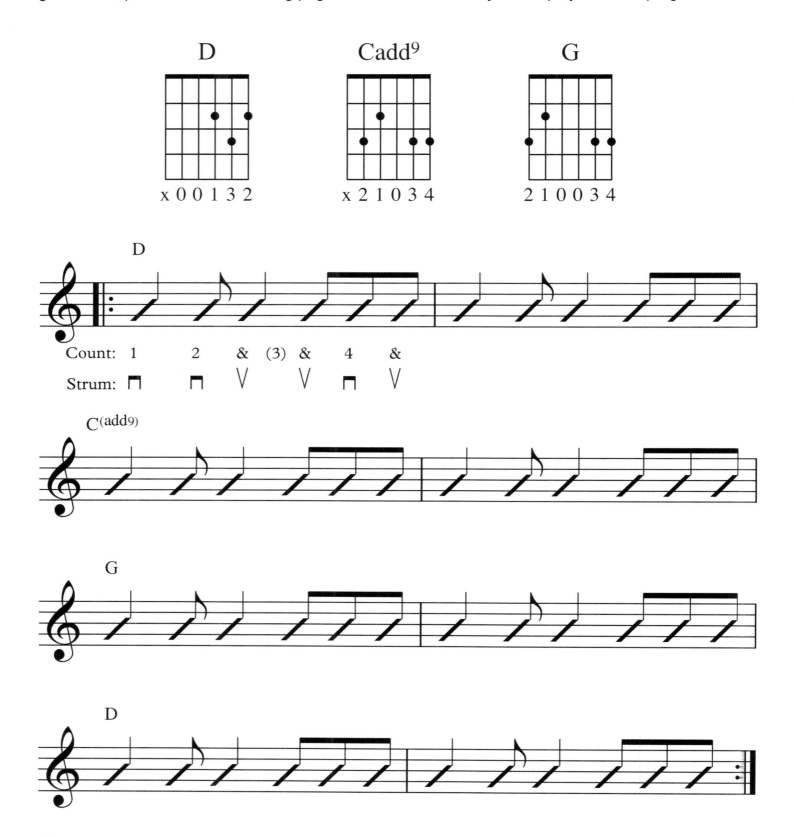

Melodic Lead

The following melodic riff within the repeat signs contains repeat brackets. The first time the riff is played, you should play the two measures underneath the 1st ending bracket. When the riff is repeated, skip the two measures underneath the 1st ending bracket and continue directly to the measures underneath the 2nd ending bracket.

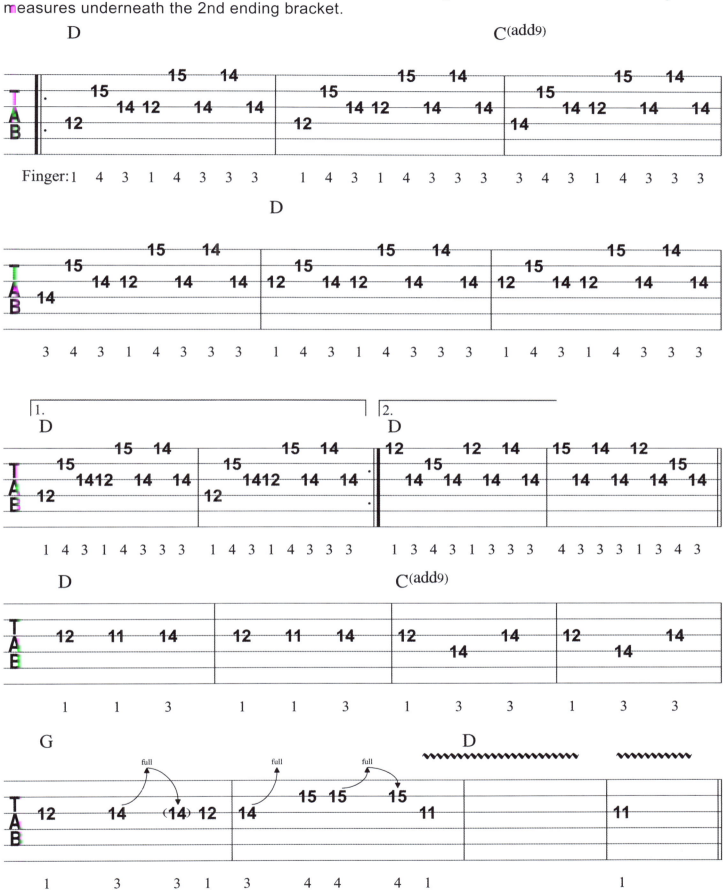

Multi-Position Lead Pattern

This lead pattern uses the A minor pentatonic scale played as a triplet lead pattern across three positions of the scale. This exercise demonstrates various ways to switch from position to position. The first two staffs show the pattern ascending; the bottom two staffs show the same pattern in reverse. Play through each example along with the metronome without stopping and gradually buildup speed.

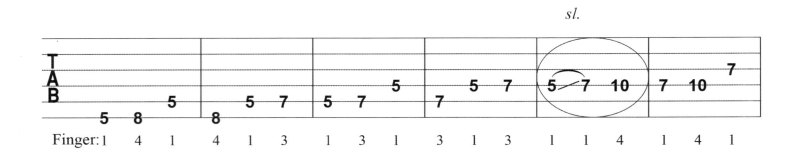

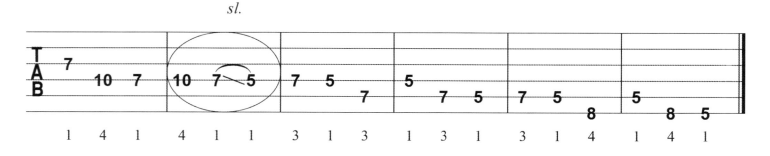

Bi-Dextral Hammer Ons

This technique introduces the right hand tap, which requires you to reach over to the neck with your right hand and hammer on the note using your right hand index or middle finger. After tapping the note, pull off with your right hand finger to the lower notes on the neck that should be fretted with your left hand fingers. The "R" above the tab staff indicates a right hand tap. This technique allows you to hammer on and pull off full arpeggios and other wide interval phrases very quickly. Right hand tapping was made popular by Eddie Van Halen, who used tapping throughout many of his famous solos.

If you tap with your middle finger, you can keep the pick in position in your hand. If you feel more comfortable tapping with your index finger, you can use a technique called "palming the pick" where you tuck the pick under your middle finger to get it out of the way. After playing the riff, bring it back into position to go back to regular picking.

The following riff is an example of what you can do with bi-dextral hammer ons. Once you're comfortable with the technique, experiment with it at different frets and on different strings. You can also do other fun things with this technique, such as bending a note in your left hand and then tapping a note above it while holding the bend. This bend and tap technique was made popular by Billy Gibbons.

```
  R P H  R P H  R P H  R P H        R P H   R P H   R P H   R P H
||--9-2-5--9-2-5--9-2-5--9-2-5--.||--10-2-5--10-2-5--10-2-5--10-2-5--.||
||------------------------------.||---------------------------------.||
||------------------------------.||---------------------------------.||
||------------------------------.||---------------------------------.||

Finger:  R 1 4  R 1 4  R 1 4  R 1 4     R 1 4  R 1 4  R 1 4  R 1 4


  R P H   R P H   R P H   R P H         R P H   R P H   R P H   R P H
||--10-4-7--10-4-7--10-4-7--10-4-7--.||--12-4-7--12-4-7--12-4-7--12-4-7--.||
||----------------------------------.||----------------------------------.||
||----------------------------------.||----------------------------------.||
||----------------------------------.||----------------------------------.||

  R 1 4  R 1 4  R 1 4  R 1 4          R 1 4  R 1 4  R 1 4  R 1 4
```

Natural Minor Scales

Many modern Rock and Blues players have incorporated the use of full natural minor scales into their soloing. The pentatonic scales you've already learned are abbreviated versions of the regular major and minor scales. The pentatonic scales contain five notes; the natural minor scale contains seven notes. The word "natural" refers to the fact that the scale is in its original unaltered state. The A natural minor scale is particularly unique because this key contains all natural notes (no sharp or flat notes). The notes in an A natural minor scale are A - B - C - D - E - F - G. The natural minor scale can be used to create more complex and interesting melodies.

Below are the five basic positions of the A natural minor scale shown ascending and descending. The root notes have all been circled on the staff and scale diagrams.

1st Position A Minor Scale

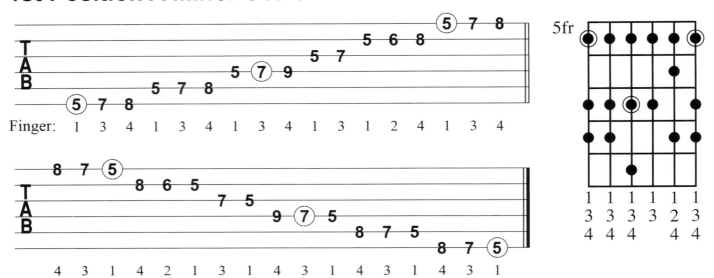

2nd Position A Minor Scale

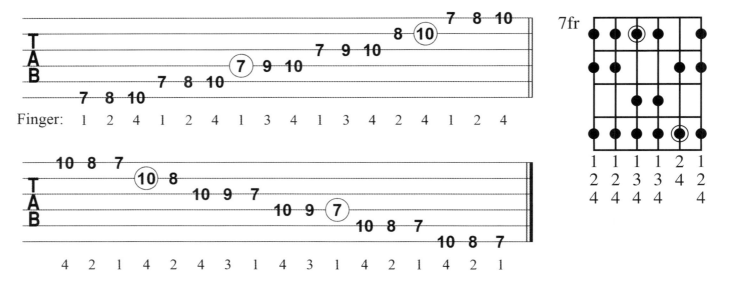

3rd Position A Minor Scale

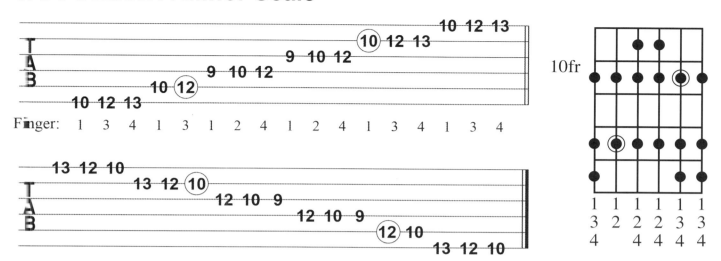

4th Position A Minor Scale

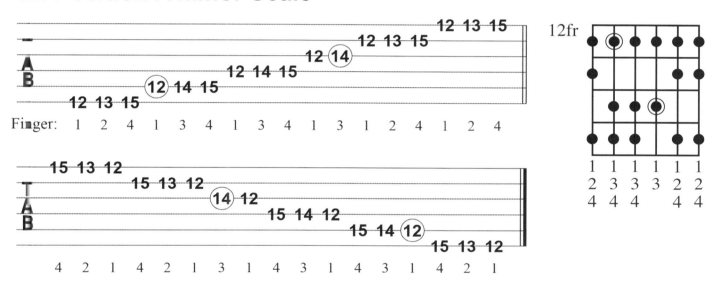

5th Position A Minor Scale

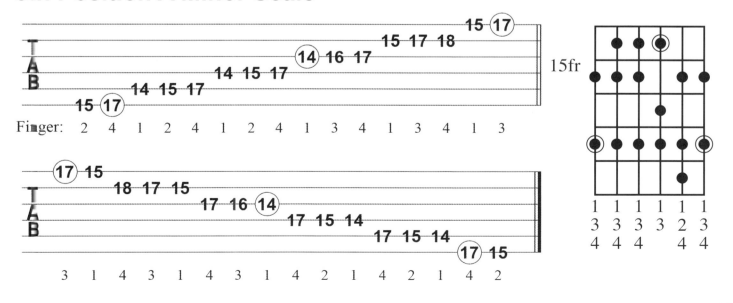

A Natural Minor Fretboard Diagram

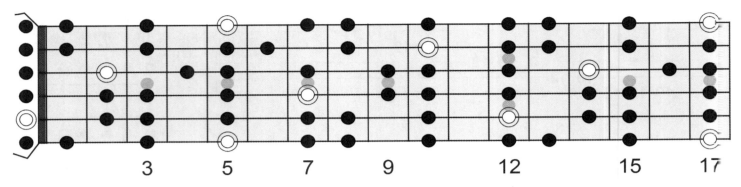

Drop D Tuning

Drop D tuning refers to lowering the pitch of the 6th string from E to D. This gives the guitar a heavier, meaner sound. Drop D has been used for years in hard rock and heavy metal, so much so that many bands have written their entire catalogs in Drop D.

To tune your guitar to Drop D tuning, strike the open 4th string (D) and the open 6th string together. Gradually lower the 6th string from E to D until the 4th and 6th strings sound "in tune" with each other. These two strings are now both tuned to D an octave apart from each other. You can check your tuning using the online tuner at RockHouseMethod.com to make sure you've got it.

Rhythms are extremely easy to play in Drop D because the 6th string power chords are now played with just one finger. Simply bar one finger across the lowest three strings at any fret. You can also play a D5 chord just by strumming the lowest three open strings. Below are three chord diagrams to give you some ideas on how to use Drop D tuning to play chords.

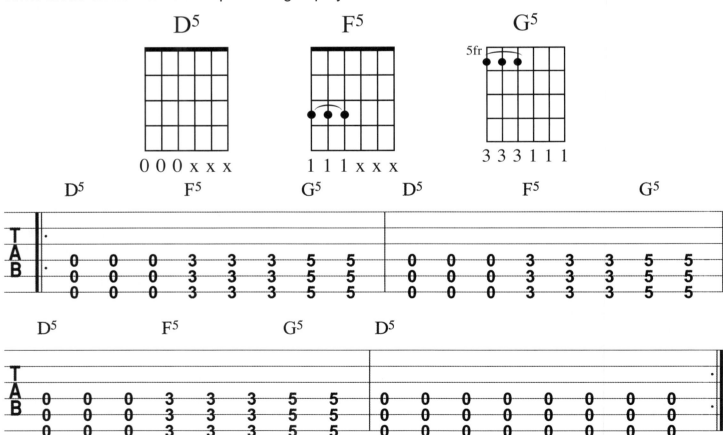

You can solo over the rhythm you've just learned using the minor pentatonic scales in the key of D. Since the 6th string is tuned down to D, all of the 6th string notes in the scale positions have moved two frets. To avoid confusion and mistakes, you can simply avoid playing notes on the 6th string. It's also good to remember that since you are in the key of D and your 6th string is now tuned to D, the open string and the 12th fret notes are now root notes that you can easily use as well.

The following example solo uses the D minor pentatonic scale in various positions. The position changes are indicated below the staff as they happen.

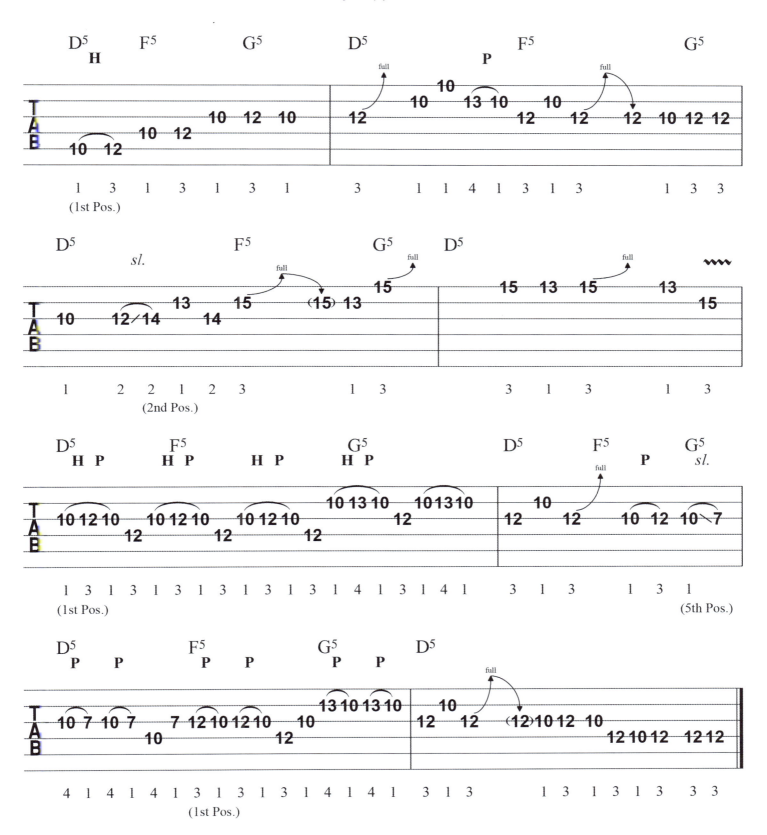

Slow Metal Rhythm & Solo

This slow metal rhythm is an arpeggiated riff in the key of Bm. Keep your left hand fingers in place, fretting the notes throughout each measure and let the notes ring out over each other as you pick them. The picking rhythm is straight eighth notes with a slow, simple feel. Once you've got the pattern memorized, play along with the bass and drum backing track.

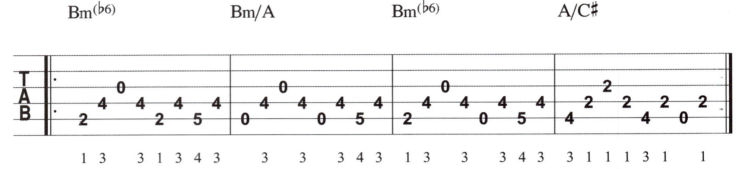

The following solo demonstrates various lead techniques learned throughout this program and can be played over the Slow Metal Rhythm. This lead is in the key of Bm and uses different positions of the B natural minor scale. You can also improvise your own lead using the B minor scales. All of the A natural minor scale positions from Lesson 14 can be transposed to the key of Bm by moving each of them two frets higher on the fretboard.

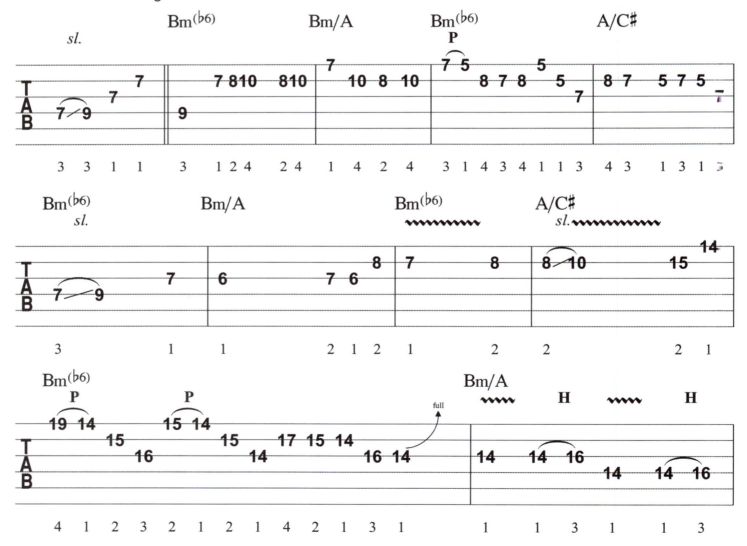

88

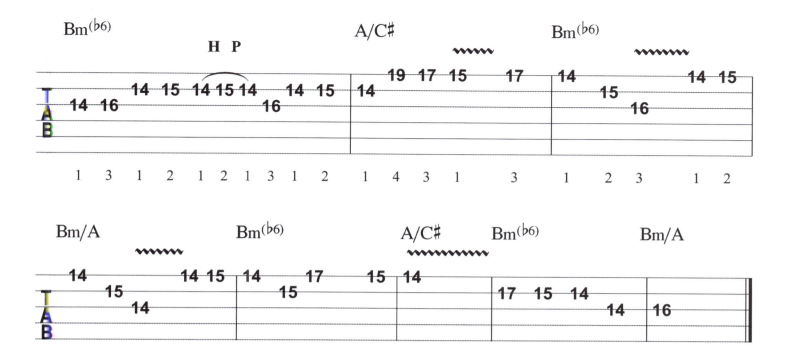

John McCarthy's
Modes Demystified
Master the Secrets of Lead Guitar

UNLOCK THE SECRETS TO TURN SCALES AND MODES INTO AMAZING SOLOS!

Designed for all skill levels by renowned guitarist John McCarthy, this program starts with learning major scale theory and how to play the major scale in every key. Easily find the relative minor key for each major scale and create master charts that are the source of leads, chord progressions and songs. John teaches all seven modes derived from the major scales and their distinct sound, which you will apply while playing over full band backing tracks. Learn passing tone theory, chordal soloing, how to create a chord scale and chord progression for each mode plus the extended positions of the seven note scale across the neck. **This program cracks the code that will intensify your guitar playing!**

Includes:
- 2 DVD's With Over 2 Hours of Instruction • Full Band Backing Tracks • Portable Device Ready Video

Review Quiz 2

1) How many different positions of the minor pentatonic scale are there?
A. Six
B. Three
C. Five
D. Seven

2) The fast shaking of a sustained note is called
A. Bending
B. A hammer on
C. Vibrato
D. A bar

3) Bar chords are
A. Moveable chords
B. Easy to play
C. Open string chords
D. Only used in jazz

4) Two frequently used lead techniques are
A. Tuning and strumming
B. Bar chords and open chords
C. Hammer ons and pull offs
D. Eighth notes and quarter notes

5) Which positions of the minor pentatonic scales can be used for playing leads?
A. None of them
B. The 4th and 5th positions
C. All five positions
D. Only the 1st position

6) Blues scales contain
A. The blues tri-tone
B. Nine different notes
C. Only open strings
D. Three bar chords

7) An arpeggio is defined as
A. A scale
B. A note that is played using vibrato
C. The notes of a chord played separately
D. The root note and the seventh

8) The note that makes a chord major or minor is
A. The fifth
B. The root note
C. The third
D. The seventh

9) The bi-dextral hammer on technique requires you to
A. Switch hands and play the guitar upside down
B. Fret all of the notes with your left hand
C. Reach over to the neck and tap notes with your right hand
D. Use distortion

10) Right hand tapping is indicated by which letter above the tab staff?
A. B
B. R
C. S
D. H

11) When tapping with your right hand index finger, move the pick out of the way by
A. Palming the pick
B. Dropping the pick
C. Putting the pick down
D. Holding the pick between your teeth

12) How many different letter name notes are in the natural minor scale
A. Five
B. Three
C. Eight
D. Seven

13) To play in Drop D tuning,
A. Use a distortion pedal
B. Drop D guitar on D floor
C. Tune the guitar's 6th string down to D
D. Tune every string on the guitar to D

14) You can fret power chords in Drop D tuning by using how many fingers?
A. Five
B. One
C. Four
D. Seven

15) Transpose the A natural minor scale positions to the key of B minor by moving each position
A. Two frets higher
B. Two frets lower
C. Five frets higher
D. Seven frets lower

16) Which of the following is not a lead technique?
A. Hammer ons
B. Bends
C. Bi-dextral hammer ons
D. Bar chords

Answers on Page 96

Changing a String

Old guitar strings may break or lose their tone and become harder to keep in tune. You might feel comfortable at first having a teacher or someone at a music store change your strings for you, but eventually you will need to know how to do it yourself. Changing the strings on a guitar is not as difficult as it may seem and the best way to learn how to do this is by practicing. Guitar strings are fairly inexpensive and you may have to go through a few to get it right the first time you try to restring your guitar. How often you change your strings depends entirely on how much you play your guitar, but if the same strings have been on it for months, it's probably time for a new set.

Most strings attach at the headstock in the same way; however electric and acoustic guitars vary in the way in which the string is attached at the bridge. Before removing the old string from the guitar, examine the way it is attached to the guitar and try to duplicate that with the new string. Acoustic guitars may use removable bridge pins that fasten the end of the string to the guitar by pushing it into the bridge and securing it there. On some electric guitars, the string may need to be threaded through a hole in the back of the body.

Follow the series of photos below for a basic description of how to change a string. Before trying it yourself, read through the quick tips for beginners on the following page.

Use a string winder to loosen the string.

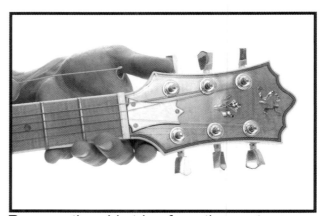

Remove the old string from the post.

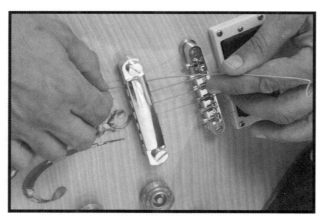

Pull the string through the bridge and discard it.

Remove the new string from the packaging and uncoil it.

Thread the end of the new string through the bridge.

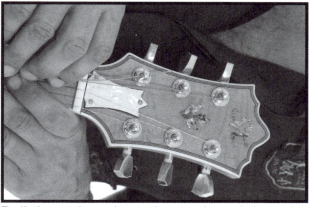
Pull the string along the neck and thread it through the small hole on the tuning post.

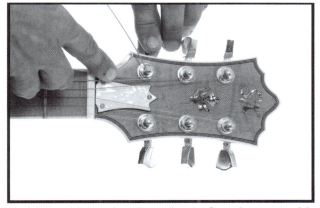
Hold the string in place just after the nut with your finger and tighten up the slack in the string with the machine head.

Carefully tighten the string and tune it to the proper pitch.

You can cut the old string off the guitar but you may want to unwind it instead and save it as a spare in case you break a string later.

Check to make sure you have the correct string in your hand before putting it on the guitar. The strings may be color coded at the end to help you identify them.

Be sure to wind the string around the tuning post in the proper direction (see photos), and leave enough slack to wind the string around the post several times. The string should wind around the post underneath itself to form a neat coil.

Once the extra slack is taken up and the string is taught, tune it very gradually to pitch, being careful not to overtighten and accidentally break the new string.

Once the string is on the guitar and tightened up, you can cut the excess string sticking out from the tuning post with a wire cutter. The sharp tail end that is left can be bent downward with the wire cutter to get it out of the way and avoid cutting or stabbing your finger. Check the ends of the string to make sure it is sitting correctly on the proper saddle and space on the nut.

New strings will go out of tune very quickly until they are broken in. You can gently massage the new string with your thumbs and fingers once it's on the guitar, slightly stretching the string out and helping to break it in. Then retune the string and repeat this process a few times for each string.

Guitar Accessories

Strings & Picks

Strings and picks are both available in different gauges. Heavier gauge strings produce a thicker, fuller sound; lighter gauges are thinner, easier to bend, and great for soloing. There are many different types of picks in different thicknesses. A heavy pick may offer you more control for lead playing, but medium and light picks have a flexibility that's good for rhythm playing. A finger-pick is a type of ring that you wear on your thumb for down-picking, allowing all of your fingers to be available for more complex finger-picking. When changing your strings, you'll probably want to use a string winder. A string winder is a simple gadget that fits right over the machine heads so that you can quickly wind or unwind a string.

Strings Come In Various Styles & Gauges

Different Types of Picks Are Available

String Winders Make Changing Strings Easier

Music Stands & Metronomes

As soon as you begin your first guitar lesson, you'll notice how important it is to have a music stand. Whenever you try to learn a new song from sheet music, or even go through a lesson in this book, you'll want to have the music right in front of you where it's close and easy to read. Don't try to balance a book on your lap or read it from the floor. If you're practicing scales and exercises or working out a difficult new guitar line, you can use a metronome to set a steady practice tempo and keep yourself in time. There are mechanical or electronic models, or you can download the free one from RockHouseMethod.com and use your computer to keep time.

Cases & Stands

The two main types of guitar cases are hardshell cases and softshell cases. Hardshell cases are more expensive and have a sturdy construction designed for maximum protection during travel. A much lighter and smaller alternative to the traditional guitar case is a gig bag: a padded, zippered guitar glove that is carried over the shoulders like a backpack. Guitar stands are usually collapsible and easy to take with you, but you can also use one at home to keep your guitar on display when you're not practicing.

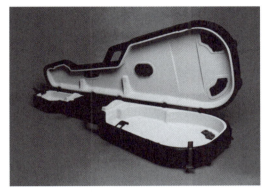
Hardshell Case

Gig Bag

Make Your Own Tool Kit

Put together your own tool kit by keeping all of the important tools and spare parts you need in one place, like a small backpack or a compartment inside your guitar case. You should always have spare strings, a string winder, picks, batteries, and any small screwdrivers or wrenches that fit your guitar. You can purchase a multipurpose tool designed especially for guitarists (sort of like a pocket knife without the knife) that contains a few different types of screwdrivers and an assortment of Allen wrenches. Some other good things to keep with you: wire cutters, fuses if your amp uses them, guitar polish and a soft cloth, music paper and pencil, and duct tape. You may also want to keep a small recording device handy to record your own musical ideas and use them to start writing your own songs.

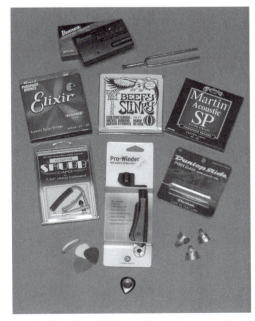
A Collection Of Important Accessories

Review Quiz Answers

Quiz 1

1) C
2) A
3) C
4) C
5) C
6) B
7) B
8) D
9) A
10) B
11) A
12) C
13) A
14) C
15) C
16) B

Quiz 2

1) C
2) C
3) A
4) C
5) C
6) A
7) C
8) C
9) C
10) B
11) A
12) D
13) C
14) B
15) A
16) D

Musical Words

Progression: A series of chords that are played within a song.

Accent: A louder pick or strum.

Dynamics: The variation of sound levels, louder and softer.

Riff: A short melody usually 2 or 4 beats long.

5th Position: The section of the guitar spanning the 5th through 8th frets across all six strings.

Triplet: A group of three notes played in the time of two of the same notes.

Natural Minor Scale: The natural minor scale has the same tones as the major scale, but uses the sixth tone of the major scale as its tonic. This changes the semitones (half steps) between the second and third tones and the fifth and sixth tones creating a scale formula of Whole – Half – Whole – Whole – Half – Whole – Whole.

Sixteenth Note: A note having the time duration of one sixteenth of the time duration of a whole note.

Syncopation: Deliberate altering of the meter or pulse of a composition by a temporarily shifting the accent to a weak beat or an off-beat.

Turnaround: A short phrase at the end of a progression that brings the player back to the beginning of the song in a smooth transition.

Arpeggio: The notes of a chord played separately.

Octave: An interval spanning seven diatonic degrees (eleven half-steps). An octave above C would be C.

Root Note: The tonic or fundamental note of a chord. The note which gives a chord or scale its letter name.

Caged System: A "five shape" contiguous sequence that spans the fretboard of a guitar based off of the C, A, G, E and D (major, minor, dominant 7th, etc.) open chord forms.

Bi-Dextral Hammer On: Also known as "tapping." Bi-Dextral Hammer Ons are performed by using the left and right hands to perform wide stretch hammer ons and pull offs.

Blues Tri-Tone: The interval of a sharped fourth (augmented fourth, enharmonically spelled as a diminished fifth). This interval was known as the "devil in music" in the Medieval era because it is the most dissonant sound in the scale. This note is usually added to a minor pentatonic scale to give it a bluesy sound.

Melody: A succession of musical tones. It represents the linear or horizontal aspect of music.

Dominant 7th Chord: A chord constructed with the 1st = 3rd – 5th – and b7 degrees of a major scale. Also known as a 7th chord.